PEREGRINE BOOKS

FICTIONS

'The novel is no more the work of imagination than it is a reflection of reality: its essence, its necessary quality lies in the connection between the real and the imaginary'

In this absorbing study of literary and social theory Michel Zéraffa examines the relationship between the novel as it delineates the author's view of society and as a subjective work of art. Drawing examples from the entire spectrum of Western literature, from Cervantes to Robbe-Grillet, he shows that while the novel possesses its own integral aesthetic logic, this logic is always congruent with the logic of society. Indeed, the social and historical dimension is always present, even in the work of such anti-traditional 'anti-social' writers as Virginia Woolf and Samuel Beckett. Zéraffa believes that the 'sociology of the novel should enable the history of a society to be read not *in* its literature but *through* its literature'. In this he provides a valuable counterweight to the Marxist strictures on the direction that the novel has taken in the West – into 'the luxury hotel of the absurd' – a direction which he considers both inevitable and authentic.

Michel Zéraffa is Director of Research in Aesthetics at the Centre National de la Recherche Scientifique and a lecturer at the University of Paris. Among his publications are *Personne et personnage* (1969), *Roman et société* (1971) – of which *Fictions* is the English translation – and *La Révolution romanesque* (1972).

FICTIONS

The Novel and Social Reality

Michel Zéraffa

TRANSLATED BY
CATHERINE BURNS AND
TOM BURNS

PENGUIN BOOKS

Penguin Books Ltd, Harmondsworth, Middlesex, England
Penguin Books, 625 Madison Avenue, New York, New York 10022, U.S.A.
Penguin Books Australia Ltd, Ringwood, Victoria, Australia
Penguin Books Canada Ltd, 41 Steelcase Road West, Markham, Ontario, Canada
Penguin Books (N.Z.) Ltd, 182–190 Wairau Road, Auckland 10, New Zealand

—

First published as *Roman et société* by Presses Universitaires de France 1971
This translation first published in Peregrine Books 1976

—

Copyright © Penguin Books Ltd, 1976

—

Made and printed in Great Britain by
Hazell Watson & Viney Ltd, Aylesbury, Bucks
Set in Monotype Plantin

Contents

CHAPTER I

The Novel as Both Literary Form and Social Institution

IN the sociology of the novel, sociology is dealing with an art. True, narrative fiction is contained within language and takes most of its own character from it; the form and content of the novel derive more directly from social phenomena than do those of other arts, except perhaps cinema; novels often seem bound up with particular moments in the history of society. We are none the less concerned with a specific art: Proust read Flaubert; Flaubert read Balzac. The works of Stendhal, James Joyce, Kafka and Faulkner have been points of reference, if not models, for whole generations of writers. The multiplicity of theories which have been propounded about the novel since the seventeenth century unquestionably confer some aesthetic status on it. Like any other art, also, the novel has its revolutionary and its conservative forms; its true *avant-gardes* and its false ones. It is divided into genres and sub-genres, all devised for the pleasure – or boredom – of various social categories of reader.

Can we, however, make any precise distinction between the novel as art and the novel as 'social manifestation'? The social aspects are so prevalent in the work of Balzac and Proust that the sociologist slips easily into thinking that his analysis of a novel will also bring to light its true aesthetic qualities. On the other hand, those who see the novel as a product of the art of writing, and, as such, independent of 'reality' are quick to accuse the sociologist of reducing the novel to its substantive content and to its genesis; they in turn will be accused by sociology of pure formalism. Are life and the history of society simply the props of the forms of fiction? Or are these forms already present in society? Critical study of the novel too often wavers between these two questions, which constitute a false dilemma.

Forms of the novel and forms of society

In fact it has been too easily forgotten that in the eyes of an artist, the notion of form concerns social reality just as much as it does the work of art itself. Neither Balzac nor Proust saw social reality as merely a mass of crude contingent facts; to borrow a phrase from Henry James, the novelist analyses the 'data' of social life, interprets them, and tries to determine their essential features in order to transmit them in writing. Consider the forewords to Balzac's *La Comédie humaine*, Joyce's *Portrait of the Artist as a Young Man*, and Henry James's *The Art of Fiction*: each of them expounds theories of the novel in which the writer insists that writing must be born from the rational observation and experience of a well-defined reality. The second-rate novelist, who tries to flatter his public, or to gratify himself with an autobiographical account (which often comes to the same thing), will either idealize reality, or devote himself to reproducing it 'as it was'. Stendhal or Faulkner, on the contrary, search for and find logical relationships between a perception of life and the composition of aesthetic forms. Original works have a revelatory function, as regards the hidden inadmissible aspects of what we call social, economic or psychological life: they are both the search for, and the expression of, their sense, or, rather, of their essence.

Notwithstanding the many obvious differences, the art of fiction has something in common with the art of painting: both are only truly significant of what is real when they are the result of an intense effort to abstract from it. Reality (and especially social reality) is no more the sum of its parts than form is a collection of techniques. For example, the a-chronological structure of Faulkner's *Absalom, Absalom* contains a whole world of longing for a past order and hatred of 'modern' society – and through that structural form, the author conveys a fundamental trait of the civilization and history of the American South. Again, Alain Robbe-Grillet, in recommending that 'time be put into parentheses', shows himself to be in the direct line of succession to Joyce, but also evokes a society which has become more and more defined in terms of specialization and spatial situation. For these two novelists the forms of reality, of mind and of art are three separate but superimposed levels of their own creation.

The works of Balzac, Dostoyevsky and Proust are both aesthetic analyses and syntheses of a reality which the novelist had already analysed and synthesized before he started to write. The paradox of the novel is the paradox of all works of art: it cannot be rendered back into the reality of which it is nevertheless the expression. But the sociologist will only be able to study the novel in terms which are totally and specifically sociological if he views it in terms of these two levels of expression, the one the thinking behind the book, the other what is written in it – and both of them possessing shape and form. A novel involves several distinct processes, each the particular concern of a particular humane study or human science. But the fact that a novel contains a variety of perspectives does not mean that a variety of critical approaches – half aesthetics, half sociology – is needed to account for them. Psychoanalysis does not stop short just at the point where sociology begins. We can view a novel as the convergence of different approaches, but only on condition that each of these achieves completeness according to its particular hypotheses and methods. Kafka's work, for example, can be judged from several angles – the sociological, the psychological, the metaphysical – which are all of them relevant and enlightening. All of them can be validly applied to every aspect of his work, including considerations of form. There is nonetheless one fact that no approach to the novel, and particularly the sociological approach, can afford to ignore without falsifying the work and its effect on its reader: the fact which consists in the nature of the art itself. The forms of fiction have their own history, which cannot be rendered in terms of history, any more than of 'society'. The sociologist who neglects this dimension of the unique character of literature and of the technicalities of fiction will be unable to perceive exactly how a novel constitutes an analytic and synthetic model of social reality. And he will also be ill-equipped for the task of explaining the effect, the impact of a novel on a society or a culture. The novelist must be considered as absolutely an artist: his work is the expression of a reality which, I repeat, already has in his mind a form and a meaning, and he expresses it by means of techniques, some of which he has inherited from his predecessors and some of which he has worked out himself from phenomena he has actually observed. Céline gave us a new view of the world by refashioning the 'trivial' modes of language which literature had previously neglected. Sartre, in turn, paid a good deal of attention to Céline's vision of the world and particularly to his mode of expressing it. Kafka's practice involved an art of linear narrative which corresponded to the one-dimensional nature of the world as he observed and experienced it. And Dos Passos could not have written *Manhattan Transfer* if he had not, first, perceived 'Manhattan' as a form which could give him a frame of reference, and, secondly, watched films and, consequently, picked up ideas about film montage. It is through its formal character, and through the techniques used to create that formal character, that a work of art exposes reality. Consequently, in order to elicit the sociological significance of the novel, it is legitimate to apply to it the methods which Francastel applied to the plastic arts: it was his comparative historian's insight into the variety of forms which enabled him to recognize the true social nature of an art, i.e. to see it as a language bespeaking society as much as spoken by society.

An even more important justification for interest in the forms of the novel is that the novel is concerned with a supremely formless reality: the reality of history, which every novel attempts to interpret. The novel is directly concerned with the nature of our situation in history, and with the direction in which that situation is about to move. Most great novelists are theorists of their art because their work poses the most insoluble of all problems of interpretation: what meaning, and therefore what form, should we give to the unceasing flow of human life? And the reason that the questions 'What is the novel?' and 'Where is the novel heading?' have arisen again and again over the last century is that the creation of a work of fiction seems – I repeat, *seems* – to imply a meaningful connection between causality and destiny: the novel should at one and the same time describe what is happening to us, extract its meaning, and signpost the direction in which we are going. (Like modern painting, the modern novel is very often accused of deforming or mutilating the human face and of presenting man as something quite distinct from anything resembling him. It is commonly said that the novel ceased to exist when the writer stopped placing his characters in a specific milieu, explaining them 'in social terms' or providing them with a clearly defined future. This assumes that the proper way to treat a character in a novel is for him first to be conditioned by society, and secondly to become its victim: the hero should thus furnish proof (mostly by dying) that society is evil – or that it is still a long way from being good. Starting from such premises, it becomes possible to treat Proust's work as a blend of narcissism and aestheticism, and to accuse Céline or Faulkner of debasing human nature.)

The novel thus assumes the guise of oracle, since more directly than other arts it confronts us openly with the issue of the meaning and value of our ineluctable historical and social condition. Implicit in the text of the novel are the propositions that man never lives by himself, and, above all, that he has a past, a present and a future. The novel's emergence as an art form affirms, essentially, that there was no society without history, nor history without society. The novel is the first art to represent man explicitly as defined historically and socially. In myth, manifestly, man is a social being but his story is only developed by obscure means, by the intervention of gods, heroes or magical events. With the novel, society enters history and history enters into society.

Society: model and counter-model

However, if man's identity within the combined framework of history and society is always present in the novel, even in novels of fantasy it is present in a positive sense in Balzac's work – and in a negative sense in Proust's. Historical and social factors are as real in *La Comédie humaine* as they are in *A la recherche du temps perdu*, but they are fundamentally real for Balzac, whereas Proust treats them purely as appearance, as secondary. The sociology of the novel cannot ignore the fact that with Flaubert, and even more so with Joyce, or Faulkner, the novel turned its back on the natural history of society as a model. It rejected the determinism on which Balzac's naturalistic world was based.

The historical development of the novel comprises two opposite tendencies: the novel was born and established itself as a genre on account of, and to account for, historical and social phenomena; it attained the status of art when it set itself over against them. It is vital to bear this in mind if we are to gauge the value of the novel as 'social representation'. We cannot, as sociologists, apply the same methods to Balzac and to Proust; social life is to be found in Balzac; it has to be searched for in Proust. In both cases proper respect has to be paid to the writer's own attitude to social phenomena; and this attitude emerges through the writing, through the style of composition. A Balzac or Dickens novel tends to begin with a scene, with something happening, and the author then goes on to relate the preceding social and historical facts; later the book resumes the tale. With Faulkner, on the contrary, such explanations develop into a kind of series of fade-ins and fade-outs in the characters' minds. These two styles of story-telling correspond directly to two particularly significant trends in the history of society.

Nevertheless Faulkner's narratives do not negate the origins of the novel, which are social and historical in the narrowest sense of the words. The novel was brought into being for men who wanted to find their place in historical continuity, and were moreover aware of constituting a certain stratum of society. So, as against the global, systematized and partly supernatural ordering propounded by myth, the novel set out to express an order established by a group in the process of instituting itself as a class, which enjoyed finding in novels explicit and chronological records of its past as well as explicit characteristics of its power, virtues and pleasures.

If we take 'art' to be a set of values inscribed in beautiful and noble form, and 'genre' to be a form of art subject to the framework of a particular set of rules, then the novel first emerged as a non-art and a non-genre. For a start, it freed itself completely from verse forms: its prose style then rapidly merged with 'the prose of social relationships', to use Hegel's phrase, and grew more and more to resemble the style of historical narrative. Nevertheless the novel soon took over from the myths whose dominance it had broken down – and to whose decline it owed its origins. Sprung from a world vision from which visionary elements were being eliminated, the novel, in turn, came to provide magical visions of life.

The history of the novel is made up of the alternation or confrontation of 'truth in fiction' with 'the falsity of fiction'.[1] For every novel in which reality is transfigured, there is almost always a novel which reduces everything to matter of fact realities. In sociological terms, this division of the novel between realism and unrealism indicates that it proffers models of life, of morals, of sentiments to different sectors of society, and that in so doing it registers their conflicts. The picaresque novel was written as a counter to *L'Astrée* and *Le Grand Meaulnes* to combat the 'social realism' which seemed dominant in 1913.[2]

However, I have been using the term 'myth' almost in the sense of illusion. For myth, taking it this time as a group of ideals or values which give meaning to reality, has always been necessary to the great achievements of the realistic novel.

But whether it idealizes existence or reveals its innermost motivations, the novel always retains its basic historical–social nature. It does so because, if we put ourselves in the place of the reader, for whom the novel is principally a succession of pages, the novel presents interpersonal relationships which are in process of development, more or less continuous but always evolutionary, always moving. A transcription of *Waiting for Godot* into novel form is perfectly conceivable, but its author would be compelled to describe in words what the actors in the play frequently express by gesture and attitude. So, translated into narrative, what was a confrontation between two isolations, would become a person-to-person relationship. Both characters would be made explicit, placed in time, and the completely static quality of expectation which Beckett obtains as playwright would be replaced by expectancy in terms of movement. At the very least, rewriting *Godot* as narrative would erode the radical difference which in other instances separates Beckett's dramatic work from his novels. His plays all develop the theme of meaninglessness, but fold back on themselves (life is fatally closed, repetitive, unchanging; it is a becalmed waiting for death, a death which, itself, does not 'arrive'). His novels are exhaustive treatments of the statement that life has no meaning. And this exhaustion ('we must speak words as long as they are still there') is linear: the ending it moves towards is its own.

Now everybody knows that there is no 'line' in Beckett's novels, and that he rejects even the idea of intention or of design. One has to be a sociologist (which is precisely my point) to detect the existence of 'real' social relationships in *Molloy*. But, sociologist or not, why read a book written to negate the very notion of historical time as if it were a story, and why find human relationships in a text which destroys even the idea of society and humanity? This unconquerable tendency to read *Molloy* 'like a novel' has two causes. Firstly, we have read the 'story' of Raskolnikov, or Leopold Bloom (Molloy's ancestor); above all, the fact is that whatever Beckett says about it, his book links people and things together, even if it is only by contiguity. Jorge Luis Borges is right: 'the central problem of the novel is causality';[3] and Barthes even more so: 'The novel, taken in its most concrete terms, is a *sociable* act; it establishes literature as an institution.'[4]

From *Petit Jehan de Saintre** to *Cousin Pons*, the novel doubly establishes literature as institution. It not only demonstrates that there is no human condition outside history or society, but also makes that circumstance explicit, and illustrates it with precise and coherent examples. The 'sociability' of the novel served to endow it with sizeable cultural, political and ideological functions. Even more than poetry, for example, fiction comes to express ideas of nationhood and national renaissance in colonies or countries which have recently gained independence. The novel as a social institution is manifest in the number of novelists awarded the Nobel Prize for literature or given academic posts, and the profoundly sociological implications of the rewards available to writers. Alain Robbe-Grillet rightly refers to the special 'mental culture' which brings to the reading of a novel the frame of mind appropriate for Balzac. To grasp the truth of Beckett's *The Unnameable*, we have to clear our minds of the historical and social conception of the human being to which Balzac's name is linked. To read Beckett, we have to free ourselves of a particular frame of reference for reading, just as we reject a particular approach to looking at paintings when we study a Mondrian, banishing the ghosts of representational art from our minds.

This frame of reference for reading (at least in the West) took six centuries to develop, i.e. the time needed for the novel to become a genre. It is true that the novel appears as a specific narrative style from the twelfth century on, but its full recognition as a literary form did not come until the end of the eighteenth century – not very long before Balzac's name came to symbolize the novel as the true expression of historical and social reality. The novel gained the uncon-

* Antoine de la Salle, 1398–1460.

tested status of a genre (in its own right) when its societal role was first recognized and, indeed, taken as the novel's proper task. Defined as 'modern bourgeois epic' by Hegel, the novel institutionalized literature by a Hegelian process which in fact led, with Balzac, to a virtual fusion of the ideas of History, Society and the State.

However, the novel's reign as both representation of, and way of getting to know, the history of society (both polarized on the dominant class) was soon broken off and contradicted by the novel's emergence as an aesthetic fact; it emerged as a work of art just when it was conceived as bound up, in substance as well as form, with historical and social phenomena. As genre, the novel embraced and expressed the causal and teleological processes of the history of society. As art, it pushed into the background the essentially sociological personality described by Diderot, Balzac, Defoe or Dickens. Flaubert's accomplishment, wrote Proust, was revolutionary. He was absolutely right. With Emma Bovary, personality is no longer either primordially social or historical; moreover, the existence of an art specific to fiction is revealed, a fact which was to confront writers with increasingly acute problems.

Naturally, the novel was both a genre and a literary art, though unacknowledged, before it became both these things explicitly and officially, so to speak. Painting developed in the same way, its specific concern long remaining 'representational' before becoming 'formal' in the twentieth century. The novel's wide variations in theme and length, the many successive stylistic changes, the sheer number of real and imaginary milieux it evokes, all encourage the feeling that it has neither rules nor laws.[5] It seems to follow a path of its own, parallel to human events, following the thread of history and, above all, taking on the characteristics of speech. Fiction as an institution is so embedded in life as a whole that there is hardly any need to make its institutional character explicit. To write down the story of one person or several people does not seem to involve any principles of composition or perspective. But nevertheless, from its first appearance the novel possessed basic norms, which defined its content and determined its modes of composition. Not, admittedly, that these norms were very precise if we compare them with the principles governing poetry, but they were real to the extent that, rooted in the forms of the mythical tale, they yet permitted the novel to be concerned with the social groups seeking to break with mythological order and thought – without making it obvious they were doing so. In decline, myth prepared frameworks of significance and of style for the novel, and the same social phenomena determining the decline of myth were formulating the first rules for the novel.

The first principle involved in the composition of fiction is the obligation to set up a finite, autonomous, historical system. Balzac illustrates the chronological approach to time (the time of his characters is the time of clocks, even during flashbacks); Proust on the contrary contrasts the true time of the mind with the artificial time of society: but both novelists articulate a world which endures; beyond its duration – beyond the last word written and read – there is nothing. One could even argue that in this sense Balzac's narrative is less closed than Proust's, since the *Comédie humaine* continues, historically and structurally, after the end of his *Splendeurs et misères des courtisanes*, whereas the word Time which ends Proust's work is a door shut on the life of the spirit and opened up to death.

The truth is that this notion of the story of a society, exalted as truth by Balzac and rejected as trickery by Proust, brings fiction to life, and to death; the hero's or the narrator's project is accomplished in terms of a progress which must of necessity be brought to a halt. Moreover, for the very reason that it seems to reproduce the movement of life and imitates the linking of causes with effects, the last line of a novel leaves us with a greater sense of irremediable ending than the end of a play. Whatever the book's ending, happy or sad, the reader never feels like the spectators of the mystery plays who wanted to assault Judas, or those who hissed the villain at melodramas.

Essentially 'social' in nature, the novel has little to do with inciting rebellion against 'society'. Because of its finite system – as opposed to the closed system of myth, to use Lévi-Strauss's expression – the novel is *par excellence* the appropriate genre from which a sociology of time and of death might be developed.

The novel has for long had rules and laws which emerged from the history of society itself, since novelists – particularly those of the Enlightenment – wished to show that society was both cause and consequence of human nature. The realism of Fielding or Marivaux derives from a conception of art which is genuinely social and historical, and which grew in opposition to the elevated notions of many authors who presented life as an idyll and their characters as perfect beings. From Defoe's *Moll Flanders* to Sade's *Justine*, this aesthetic is built up by opposition and exclusion, the novelist seeking to penetrate to the core of actual social reality through the outer coverings of the religious and political order. Rousseau also worked by contrast and exclusion when he separated out the socially real from the injustices of the contemporary order so as to translate it into a world vision which he believed to be the true, healthy, 'natural' one. So, although the laws and rules always seem to be new, re-created, the specific achievement of the genre of fiction comes about as the result and function of a sociological perception, a perception more and more precise among original writers. And this precision is further enhanced as European societies become more complex and more differentiated.

This differentiation (accompanied by a decline in 'values') eventually gave rise to a circumstance of some sociological significance, a significance all the greater in that it happened largely in reaction to fiction that was too much the prisoner of social description: from being an implicit work of art, the novel became an art in explicit terms. Flaubert and Henry James, especially, contributed to the novel's primarily aesthetic status. Nevertheless, if 'the idea of the novel as a work of art' (to quote one of James's commentators) only made its appearance and assumed dominance in the last third of the nineteenth century, it remained unconnected with any doctrine of 'art for art's sake'.[6] Henry James justified the primarily aesthetic quality which the novel must possess by the writer's need to find meaning in complex, fluid reality and, consequently, to express such meaning through a particular form. Flaubert, some time before, had hardly thought of the individual quality which the writer must give a character as intrinsic to it; the 'psychological' requirement is attached to the character's special place within a 'real' social milieu, a milieu with conventions which a sensitive person cannot but flout, and which, for its part, shuts her out. Emma Bovary both rejects and is rejected.

To claim full aesthetic status for the novel was to divert it from that correspondence with the social order for which Balzac's achievement had provided the literary model. It also meant turning away from the principles of the 'naturalist' school which, though it declined fairly rapidly in France, had a decisive influence on the European and American novel until just after the First World War. Nevertheless, in acclaiming the novel primarily as an art form, James was not merely reacting against naturalism and realism of Balzac. A direct disciple of Flaubert's, he was still a great admirer of Balzac and Zola; his main reaction, in general and basic terms, was against any attempt at some grand scheme in his perception or interpretation of reality. He was opposed to novelists who like to impose some order (which they believe to be classical, but which is actually wholly arbitrary) on psychological and social reality when their true task is to reveal its nuances and complexity underneath the apparatus of social conventions. This is the reality made manifest in James's works, delineated with a precision which carries with it the conviction that the claim he made for the novel as art also establishes its status as sociology. James actually analyses individual characters only by demonstrating the social and economic systems of which they are integral parts, but from which their 'real being' tries to escape.

For the sociologist, a good deal of interest attaches to these efforts of the self to somehow create its own social destiny; from Balzac to James, the novel moved from social description to social interpretation. The kind of character James selects (much as Balzac chose his character Vautrin) regards society as something objective, to which he belongs and which imposes 'unacceptable' constraints on him. It is not 'society', but 'the social' that the James character reflects. It is this reflection which the author's 'technical devices' portray, revealing social relationships as objective phenomena, and a character as a being, a self.

If we needed any testimony for the profoundly sociological nature of the process of interpretation and formalization which engages every original writer from Flaubert to Joyce, we would find it in this complete misunderstanding by one of James's critics: 'we must regard his novels as art rather than literature because they are not concerned with social description'.[7] This identification of literature with the sociological, and of the non-sociological with art, is significant: as is, even today, the false dichotomy of 'art' as against 'realism'.

It shows the tenacity of what has practically become a socio-literary model, developed, it is supposed, by the nineteenth-century novel. In fact, the nineteenth-century novel portrayed a society which merited the name, since it presented clearly definable categories and mechanisms – though it was only Balzac's skills that rendered them clearly discernible. Only when society came to lose its 'Balzacian' quality of organized totality – only when the novelist came to forego his claim to perceive society as a picture, or as an organism with countless distinct and exemplary ramifications to select from – did we cease to expect realism from the work of an original writer, and accord his achievement the quality of spontaneity.

This illusory sociology was created for the most part by the dominant models of nineteenth-century fiction. The trichotomy of society, history and the individual, and their interrelationships, appeared to constitute a system which could account for all human reality. The illusion governed the attitude to novel-reading and focused it principally on the character, perceived as living testimony to social and historical determinism. Alain, writing in 1925, defined the fictional character in terms of a deep-seated realism and rationality. Knowing that he belongs only to this world, and that it is the only world from which his desires can evoke any response, the hero of fiction analyses his situation by means of his own intelligence alone, journeying through the world drawing lessons from the sequence of adventures he experiences. The fictional hero never blames the gods; he feels responsible for his fate for the very reason that he does not believe in Fate. Similarly, E. M. Forster, in his remarkable *Aspects of the Novel*, written about the same time, emphasized the essentially explicatory role of the novel: 'novels can solace us; they suggest a more comprehensible and thus a more manageable human race . . .'[8] The novel clarified, perhaps organized, the human condition, individual and social, which in real life seemed to be utterly incoherent.

Yet at the same time that Alain and Forster were putting the emphasis on the congruence of logic, order and narrative form in the novel, a new generation of writers (Proust, Joyce, Virginia Woolf, Alfred Döblin) was rejecting this function of reassurance in fiction, and in particular for its characters: for they cannot be true unless they are represented as lost, uncertain, hesitant, astonished, in a world which has become utterly kaleidoscopic. Far from having to 'make sense of life', the novel and its characters present interpersonal relationships which seem to become turbulent and atomistic immediately they are disengaged from conventions, ritual behaviour and constraints – i.e. from formal social relationships. *Men* have, unfortunately, a past, and an inhuman one: but, fortunately, *man* has a future: a genuine capacity for development. Over against the fated actuality of the individual should be contrasted his true self, as realized in direct interaction with others and with himself. Far from consoling the reader by giving him the comfort, bounded by mortality as it is, of a rational order, the novel's role is to evoke the essentially non-finite quality of existence. Thus the models established by Balzac, Tolstoy or Dickens become useless for later writers who want to represent a world where even the notions of order and hierarchy have foundered, and where authentic 'values' are to be found only in our thought processes. The writer can no longer, wrote Proust, analyse social reality in terms of 'gross dimensions of social phenomena', but through penetrating 'deep into the nature of an individuality'.

In adopting a vision of the world dominated by uncertainty, by risk, by possibility, Proust or Joyce were not divesting the novel of social reality. They are concerned every bit as much as Balzac with social reality, but their originality rests in their denying that structure, or 'history', or the mechanisms of society can provide man with referents which can enable him to know himself and the world. One of the most basic differences between *La Comédie humaine* and *A la recherche du temps perdu* is that in one, man only exists in terms of how he acts upon and within the world, whereas in the other his actions are virtually deprived of value. But the fact that in Joyce's *Ulysses* truth is separated from the very notion of social and historical reference – and attached to interior life, to immediate personal experience – is still, and this is Joyce's view too, a sociological phenomenon.

Yet it remains true that in Proust the novel retains its rational nature, and for two good reasons: the disorder of the Verdurin group (set up to disintegrate the 'order' of the Guermantes) is still a kind of order – and the Proustian narrator (like the protagonists of Gide's *Les Faux-Monnayeurs*) tries to make sense of it in his exploration of his own and others' minds. Moreover, he unmasks the realities of social relationships as rigorously as Balzac's Vautrin. The surrealists were not mistaken in seeing that the formulation in which the 'psychological' novel represented humanity was arbitrary, unrealistic and constrictive. They forgave Balzac for the elements of myth and fantasy in *La Comédie humaine*; but they condemned Proust since, in retracing the exploration of a consciousness (within the framework of a bourgeois world), his *A la recherche du temps perdu* only harnessed the forces of imagination instead of liberating them.

The surrealists' rejection of the novel is extremely significant. André Breton pointed to what was wrong about the novel: it organized living. Whether determinist or anti-determinist, the novel still integrates, organizes, harmonizes. The escapist novel, for instance, lets the reader escape into anything – except freedom; in it, desire, pleasure and, above all, imagination is reconstructed, given a different social framework, in short, 'composed'. In dealing with the whole notion of 'being with', the novel, even the Joycean novel, remained didactic. One has to wait (apart from rare exceptions like Raymond Roussel or René Daumel) until after the Second World War, and the belated influence of Kafka, for Western writers to reject the notion of the *Bildungsroman* and carry the 'asocial' novel to the limits of unmeaningfulness. Sade's *Juliette*, as M Blanchot observes, belongs to the class of 'didactic' novels. Though quite properly revered by surrealists and by all those who see any social order as oppressive, it nevertheless shows itself to be characteristic of the didactic novel. For how could that novel possibly convey, as it does, the impression of moral transgression, or of revolutionary intention, if it did not constitute a code, a manifesto for human relationships founded on the complementarity of pleasure and pain, and yet integrated in a real social order of an especially hierarchical kind? For Sade really seems to be reproaching the dominant class with not exploiting its powers to the full in the realm of pleasure.

Sade, therefore, obtains one of the most powerful effects of subversion in any culture, and constructs at the same time a social apparatus with at least as much rigour as Balzac – and the same applies to Laclos. On the other hand, Proust and Joyce decompose the social apparatus in order to promote subjective reality and truth. Yet this reversal still leaves them prisoners of the social order, since the narrator of *A la recherche du temps perdu* and the central figure of *Ulysses* are always using everyday life and the concreteness of social relationships (of which they are both witnesses and victims) as points of reference in order to discover their true selves. Stendhalian or Proustian, the novel stays within the framework of social discourse. The logic of social relations still provides the units of measurement for it.

Still from a surrealist viewpoint, let us look at the stories of Beckett or Robbe-Grillet. Though drained of all historical circumstance or logical coherence, there remains none the less activity within the framework of the social. The characters in these stories speak or have spoken to others; they make use or have made use of objects; they are, or are not, like Molloy, 'in my mother's room'; and so they are part of a perfectly identifiable social system. Complicity in a social order is theirs, in spite of themselves.

Since the most anti-social novel retains social aspects, it is only to be expected that the novel is less easily accorded the specific status of art than, say, painting. Nevertheless the 'new novel' produced a shock in France which was comparable to that produced by abstract art. But already, during the 1920s, *Ulysses* and Virginia Woolf's *Jacob's Room* had been considered as 'cubist' works, in the pejorative sense of the word. In the same way that so-called traditional painting, superseded in turn by impressionism, cubism and abstract art, always had as its essential point of reference the representation of the human face, so the art of fiction, the model for which Balzac had established, was basically characterized by its expressing the coherence of the individual personality, unveiled little by little through a story which one could justly call discursive. And the 'cubist' novel astonished and scandalized its readers all the more in that it portrayed and dealt with human behaviour. Its characters exist, think and speak as if they belonged to the real world. However explicitly or skilfully a novelist avoids rationality, or the continuity of Balzac or Stendhal, the substance that he works on is still our daily life. Consequently his effrontery is less easily forgiven than that of the so-called *avant-garde* painter or musician. One does not tamper with the line of humanist fiction, extending from *La Princesse de Clèves* to Zola's *Germinal*, with impunity. Yet, this humanist tradition is an illusion. Both Mme de La Fayette and Zola contravene social reality in their books as much as they contravene art.

In spite of its invincibly 'institutional' aspects, innovative fiction must be considered in terms of a very important sociological fact: it attempts a work of art. New forms, new thinking, always more or less contradict the model imprinted on the mind of the public by previous works, which had themselves been considered daring when they first appeared. No sooner have people become used to Monet, than Picasso appears. No sooner has Kafka come to be acclaimed, than Beckett intervenes.

The history of twentieth-century literary criticism is marked by perpetually nostalgic longing for the reappearance of Julien Sorels, Prince Andreis or Raskolnikovs. But Dos Passos, Bernanos, or Nathalie Sarraute cannot possibly satisfy this nostalgia if they wish at the same time to develop themselves as artists and present interpretations of significant (and consequently new) aspects of the 'society' of their time. However, this nostalgia is always sated by a flood of novels rooted in the conceptual scheme of a biography – just as representational art always related to concepts of expression or perspective. In general, these novels present the career of a character (often the author himself) as the unknown quantity of an equation in which the known constants are psychological and social.

Most discussion of the novel is tinged with a certain longing for healthy normality: all seems to be lost if the novel does not affirm the existence of human continuity, where the past engenders the present and the present in turn carries the seeds of the future. The truth of the matter is that the aesthetic viewpoints of Joyce and Beckett would be more easily acceptable if, in the labyrinths of *Ulysses* and *Molloy*, supernumerary characters wandered about who were plainly linked to the world by love, friendship, morality, some political involvement or even an avowal of their loneliness.

In fact, there cannot be a reasonable sociology of the novel unless it is recognized from the start that there are two kinds of approaches, the one appearing to carry on the realist tradition and the other seemingly bearing the stamp of artistic creation. The opposition and incompatibility of these two approaches became particularly obvious when Joyce erupted into literature, but it has grown since. Innumerable novels, often by very gifted authors, gain favour from the mass of middle-class readers because of their realism and humanism; they tell someone's story. On the other hand, the works of Robbe-Grillet, and of Henry Green in England, are known only to a relatively restricted intelligentsia – whose tastes, as we know, are followed with interest by the 'cultivated' middle classes. But it is the 'new novels' and the books by someone like Gombrowicz, that get essays, memoirs and theses devoted to them.

Like *Ulysses* round about 1930, *Le Voyeur* crystallized a conception of the novel for the 1960s. The name of Robbe-Grillet carries an implication as ambiguous, in its own way, as Picasso's. In *Gommes* he broke with an apparrently continuous cultural tradition at the same time as representing an extreme point of cultural development. This ambiguity is reflected in François Mauriac's verdict, according to which the development of the novel was from now on joined with that of painting; painting, too, had lost its aim, i.e. the representation of man in all his complexity. Yet at the same time the 'new novel' was taken to represent something completely different. These new forms of narrative, from which humanity and humanism seemed to have been emptied out, were in reality extremely representational: in spite of their authors' intentions they represented man faithfully – but dehumanized man. Did the artistic achievement of a Robbe-Grillet mean that the novel could no longer perform its mission – or, on the contrary, that it performed it only too well?[9] Like Joyce's work in 1930, the appearance of the new fiction posed a serious sociological problem: considered as 'modern' art, was not the novel both index and symptom of kinds of alienation that were even more in evidence in 1950 than they had been twenty-five years earlier?

Academicism and subversion

We can examine this problem logically only if we begin by admitting that there was always a conception of realist fiction as art. This idea, since the end of the nineteenth century, has grown more and more closely linked to the intention of writers, which is to defy, if not to subvert, the established order. Flaubert, Joyce and Faulkner wrote so that fiction should stop being a matter of 'literary activity' (in institutional terms) and become 'social action'. *Ulysses*, Lowry's *Under the Volcano*, *Molloy*, Gombrowicz's *La Pornographie*, were all worked out in opposition to the institution of the novel and, consequently, in opposition to conventions, conformity, accepted ideas and oppression. When Proust refused to write a novel which would be the kind of job-lot admired by society; when a character in *Manhattan Transfer* describes life as a subway interchange; when 'K' dies 'like a dog' – society is rejected as a viable order if not as a reality. For Dos Passos and Kafka, for Musil and Faulkner, social reality is literally fatal to man and humanity. But their protest would have stayed a dead letter if these novelists had not expressed this offence against society by means of forms in themselves offensive to the established order and official culture.

Nevertheless the sociologist needs to recognize that this sort of confrontation – both realistic and artistic – has faded or revived according to the succession of literary periods. It was only towards 1930 that Sade started to become an emblem of subversion. After the Second World War, the French right-wing intelligentsia set the lucidity, the freedom, and the critical and individualist spirit of Stendhal and of his style in opposition to politically committed literature – whereas left-wing intellectuals looked up to Faulkner, but were split into admirers and opponents of Kafka. Gide's classicism, the mirror of 'spontaneous action' (*acte gratuit*), was corrosive in 1912 but not fifty years later; and today Flaubert's *Bouvard et Pécuchet* seems more subversive than *Ulysses*.

But the further we move into the twentieth century, the greater the tension which the novelist-artist seems to feel between the imperatives of his art and his desire to express what is true, i.e. to make meaningful choices from the reality he observes. In Robbe-Grillet's work, this truth rests in the way we view things and not, as has too often been said, in things themselves. For Nathalie Sarraute truth is no longer the image of the person which a Tolstoy could still locate with precision, but only our search for selves. It becomes more and more difficult to resolve the opposition between form and truth when writers first refuse to present their public with coherent and 'consolatory' (to take up Forster's phrase) stories, and then wish to take as their subject a zone of reality which eludes the multifarious sources and channels of information or knowledge currently available to us. Reality imposes far stronger constraints on the novelist of the 1960s than on the novelist of the 1920s. The wide range of psychological, social, historical and ideological subject-matter which was for a long time the novel's province is today an encumbrance to the writer who wishes to combine authenticity and artistic endeavour. And doubtless he will find it far harder than the painter or musician to live up to his wish to criticize the social order, or to condemn it as radically as possible. A piece of kinetic art, concrete or computer music, and, now, a certain kind of film, probably transmit better than a book this refusal to come to terms with the social and moral order which is, fundamentally, common to both Flaubert and Beckett.

It is possible that Robbe-Grillet's *Le Voyeur* and *La Jalousie*, or *Molloy*, or Gombrowicz's *Ferdiduke* represent a world which has become dehumanized and that these novels consequently call the socio-political order responsible for this dehumanization to account. But the sociologist who wants to study the correspondences or contradictions between literature and the established order must pay most attention to the effect of offence or subversion which a new novel form is designed to produce.

True literature, says Georges Bataille, is linked to Evil. I wanted to insist on this dimension of 'aesthetic affront' before sketching out the problems of contemporary sociological approaches to the novel.

CHAPTER 2

Sociologies of the Novel

Ulysses, *The Sound and the Fury* and *Monsieur Ouine* deal with much more forceful social, political and ideological confrontations than does *La Chartreuse de Parme*. Again, the ostensible absence of human content in Beckett's novels is more likely to worry the reader than the notorious 'impassivity' ascribed to Flaubert. Yet there has always been something disturbing about the art of the novel, mostly because of the way in which it concentrates essentially on the individual. Even the literature that is richest in sociological content and meaning thrusts society, social life and social relationships into the background, making their presence felt in the persons of specific individuals. Balzac conveys the sense of a particular society through the presentation of a whole keyboard scale of personalities; Faulkner demonstrates the deterioration of 'Southern' society through such characters as Quentin Compson, Christmas or Colonel Sutpen.

It is always the individual who provides, and reflects, the novel's social dimension. There seem to be very few novels which do not imply that society is inevitably reducible to individuals. If one can speak of patterns of *cultural* consumption of the place of the novel seems to be defined by the way in which it conducts the solitary reader through the history of a single person or of several persons who end up by detaching themselves from the social group; they stand out from it like figures in the foreground of a picture. Even by grading his characters according to whether they are subsidiary or central, a novelist presents a fundamental critique of society. The very existence of a Cousin Pons and a Schmucke, an 'I' and a

Charlus, raises questions about our human situation and about our
nature as social beings.

Of course Beckett or Robbe-Grillet can be regarded as the archetypal nihilists of the novel, erasing society, going to the logical
extreme of giving their characters the status of mere indefinite
pronouns. But another kind of nihilism is present in Balzac. Indeed,
Balzac's subversiveness lies not only in his demonstration that
society, at every level, in all its aspects, involves an inescapable
determinism; it lies also in the way in which he 'desocializes' the
world, which he represents as a machine, with individuals playing
the parts of its managers, slaves or cogs. The more emphasis Balzac
puts on typification, the more he devalues the Society to which he
is so deeply attached, deprives it of reality, even. For in each one of
his 'types' the social mechanism can be seen at work – either destroying or catalysing feelings, ideas and values to such an extent that to
the reader the 'type' is less a representative than a ghostly manifestation of society. Although Balzac's novels are based on the
hypothesis that the individual is essentially a social being, the novels
themselves seem to demonstrate the opposite – society only exists in
so far as individuals do *not* embody (the English would say
'exemplify') society, but merely have its form and its processes traced
out on their minds and souls, for good or ill.

The character: a symbolic individual

It is equally wrong to regard the novel as a field in which society and
the individual represent two opposing poles. Such an opposition only
existed when the writer had a clear and distinct conception of the
contrast, in terms of antagonism or of complementarity. The dualism
of individual and society is the product of a period distinguished by
an increasingly positivist and deterministic world-vision. From
Marianne to *Cousin Pons* we are told that everything individual is
social, and vice versa. But Stendhal was already destroying this
'dialectic'. No hero sees himself as more individually social, and
socially individual, than does Julien Sorel. But once imprisoned, he

realizes that it is his 'self' and not his quality as an individual that has gradually separated him from society. In this moment of revelation Julien finds himself no longer an individual, but a 'being'.

The closer one comes to the period of the modern novel, with Flaubert, Meredith, James, Melville and Conrad, the more one finds the 'self' becoming the central term of fiction, a third force between two incompatible realities. In the novels of Proust, Virginia Woolf, Thomas Mann or Dos Passos one finds that the 'individuality' of the character or of the narrator lies in the very fact that they can no longer be individuals – members of a social group. Their basic attachment to the 'self' as the sole authentic human value demonstrates that they are characters who are not the creatures of a Balzacian society, where the individual was related to society as a word is to a sentence.

We use the same term 'character' for an individual like Vautrin in whom the relationship between individual and society becomes almost a merging of one into the other, and for another like Charlus, who expresses the antagonism between the self and the world. The word is also just as applicable to the protagonist in one of Jean Cayrol's novels who becomes a kind of phantom in order to retain his humanity in an inhuman world, and again to the person in Le Voyeur who is defined only in vacuo. So, whether he is designed to mirror social reality or to dissolve it, the fictional character remains symbolic, in both senses of the term: a synthesis of two distinct signs, and the image (imaginary projection) of that synthesis. The primary requirement of this symbolism is for the novelist, especially one like Balzac, to reverse Marx's sociological axiom concerning social reality, which was to the effect that an individual cannot express or represent through himself all the aspects of the social structure or of social relationships, but on the contrary, is revealed as the creature instead of the creator (conscious or unconscious) of any particular social process.[1]

Hence, while in the real world the individual is the end-product of society, in fiction the individual seems to be the mirror of society – and there is some significance in the fact that the term 'mirror' is so often used in relation to the novel and its characters. The mirror, however, is not invented ('created') by the novelist: it reflects something real. When it yields a stereotyped or sublimated image of reality (and to idealize reality is often to blacken it) it is because the writer sees men and things in terms of a class ideology. When a writer tries to represent interpersonal relationships in terms of reflections of 'society' and of 'social types', however, what we seem to be left with is a broken mirror. Reality described by Flaubert, James, Conrad, Proust or Joyce might be called interstitial. These writers seek to read between the lines of social phenomena, and it is in this reading that the sociological value of their work lies. The progressive impoverishment of character corresponds to the increasingly total disintegration of the idea of society as Balzac conceived it.

While accepting the symbolic nature of the fictional character one must also realize that the subversive, aggressive or critical role thrust on him by the author derives from illusion, or at any rate, from myth. The revulsion felt in Rastignac's outcry against Paris after having seen Goriot die is purely a matter of form. In a single moment, through one action, society seems superlatively real, and all human values deprived of reality. The revulsion displayed by Julien Sorel in the scene in his cell is no less illusory. Instead of being, like Rastignac, motivated simply by the desire for worldly success, Stendhal's hero commits the error of filling his thoughts and dreams with ambition. Roused from his dreams, he realizes in prison the happiness of feeling more alive, though about to die, than the society that had cast him out. At the end of *Remembrance of Things Past*, the narrator sees the true reality of social Time almost overcoming the true reality of Eternity, which he has spent his whole life in trying to establish. And lastly, with Kafka, the critical illusion of fiction reaches its highest level. The persistence shown by his heroes in seeking out a life and a humane order they can regard as authentic is both tragic and ludicrous. All the fictional characters who inscribe themselves lastingly in our culture are creatures who become the instruments of revelatory shocks – while behind them 'real' society marches on mechanically, continuing after they are gone.

Subjectivism and alienation

Balzac's disenchantment effects are, however, less illusory than what one finds in *Ulysses*. Proust's statement that what was 'action' before Flaubert became 'impression' after him, is profoundly true.[2] Rastignac, Gervaise or Raskolnikov do embody an active direct existential criticism of social life, in which at the same time they are participating. On the other hand, the heroes of *Ulysses* or of *The Magic Mountain* conduct their criticism of society almost entirely within the confines of their own consciousness. If one compares the final episode of *Le Rouge et le noir* with the last pages of Joyce's novel one finds that Molly Bloom's inner monologue (in which Balzac's social reality is ground and mixed into a kind of paste) challenges the social system more radically than do Julien Sorel's reflections in prison. On the other hand, Joyce's subversiveness is more factitious than Stendhal's criticism – Julien is, after all, going to be executed the next day.

The sociologist is therefore correct in regarding Marivaux, Tolstoy and Zola as authentic interpreters of the social reality of their time. Even if their characters, 'involved' in the world as they are, speak in a fictional language different from the language of historical reality, these two languages are still related to the same code, comprehending, for example, class conflict and the multiplicity of contradictions between the dreams of the individual and the determinism that rules society. Whether they live out the ideology, or the myths, of a social milieu, whether they undergo the servitude we now call alienation or try to resolve the conflicts and contradictions of an entire society by working through their individual destiny to the bitter end, even to death, these characters are not just bearing testimony to a period symptomatic of it. They imply the existence of a true parallel between society and the novel. The forms and the actions of the one provide a model for the forms and actions of the other.

When, however the 'impressionist' heroes, Leopold Bloom, Clarissa Dalloway and even some of Conrad's characters, seem satisfied with resolving such conflicts within and through their inner lives, one wonders whether Joyce is not speaking a purely fictive language which may be the unwitting product and reflection of the ideology of the dominant ruling class. Although they were unaware of the true motive forces in the society which they were describing, Balzac and Tolstoy yet recognized the mechanisms and the concrete and visible determinants of action. On the other hand a Joycean consciousness of reality based on the disintegrating power of the interior monologue may be regarded as false consciousness. Beckett's consciousness may be perceived as even more false, since the author of *Molloy* regards himan beings as literally interchangeable, and presents life as the repetitive expectation of a death, which, all the same, never comes. Thus, it is possible to read Balzac while Joyce, Beckett or Robbe-Grillet have to be deciphered, perhaps even decoded. Once they are decoded, however, they are revealed as more truly realistic than Tolstoy or Dostoyevsky for, in analysing *Ulysses* or *Molloy*, it is possible to uncover the language which a class uses to mask its real interests and motivations, which are economic in nature and arise from the will to power.

What I am trying to point out is that a continuity, or parallel, exists between the sociological analysis of the novel and the historical development of the novel. The novelist today is no longer regarded as someone concerned with the description of social and psychological phenomena. The sociologist is more concerned with the writer's conception of social life, and, consequently, with his class situation and his class consciousness.

This change of perspective (due primarily to Georg Lukács) has been incorporated progressively in the forms of the novel. Contemporary studies, however, which set out to discover the sociological truths expressed (or hidden) in writings, do not appear to be much concerned either with the methods which the writer himself employs to interpret social reality or with the particular standpoint from which he chooses to make his analysis. If solid ground is to be found on which one can base a sociological examination of the novel, one has to consider the problem from the point of view of the narrator. If one wants to display features of sociological thought in the development of the novel from Balzac to Beckett (with their 'truths' and their 'errors') one should examine the succession of roles taken by novelists as narrators. If the writer is interpreting social life, what methods are available in practice, and consequently, artistically, for this interpretation? True or false, the social consciousness of Conrad,

Joyce or Nathalie Sarraute depends, at least in the first place, on a particular objective state of socio-economic relationships. The essential question, nevertheless, is how the writer, starting from these conditions, of which he is more or less aware, can grasp what he believes to be the essential truth of a complex of interpersonal relationships. The historical dimension is necessary to any sociology of art. Genetic structuralism is founded on the structural evolution of the novel.

In the first place, one must remember that, as far as the novel is concerned, society is an essentially middle-class notion. As the middle class increased in numbers and power, so novelists saw society, or, at any rate, social man, as more and more the subject of description and criticism and were more and more taken up with the idea of society in its entirety. But, as we shall see later, this sense of universality in the novel implies the certainty – common to Marivaux, Goethe and Rousseau – that the more 'society' expands the further it is on the road toward progress and happiness. This universal social order was achieved, but was described by Balzac with a cynical detachment which would have discouraged and alarmed his predecessors – with the exception perhaps of Sade and of Laclos. For Goethe and Rousseau the word 'society' (which was always written by the self-assured Balzac with a capital S) comprehended the individual person, humanity and humanism. Naturalism was to show that, by dealing with aspects of humanity that Balzac neither could nor wished to see, his work was at once all-encompassing and partial. During the same period in which Zola was devoting himself to completing Balzac's *Comédie humaine* (and turning it upside down) Flaubert and Henry James were disowning both the reality and the idea of society as an entirety.

It is no longer society but social milieux which Henry James regarded as settings for true-to-life psychological dramas. James came to assimilate the idea of personality with that of consciousness, but a consciousness which had to be formed by contact with others. For him individuality could only flourish and grow in stature and in intelligence by virtue of the kind of social experience that may be called anti-Balzacian; for in Balzac's novels no one gains experience through society. It was society itself which, through the medium of the omniscient and all-powerful novelist, experiences individuals as

objects. James, however, following Flaubert, transfers the lessons
learned by his principal characters from their experience of others
into contributions to 'psychological insight'. But this experience is
itself a part of the history of a specific society. The psychological
distinctions, which constitute the theme of *The Golden Bowl* or of
The Ambassadors, and which condition the way in which they are
written are the outcome of social distinctions clearly understood and
described by the novelist. In all James's novels we see, first, the way
in which the bourgeoisie constitutes a social class, with conventions,
values and interests of its own and, secondly, that this social collectivity is made up of a wide diversity of individuals, which itself is a
consequence of the prevailing liberal economic system. Henry
James's universe, foreshadowing Proust's, is both closed and open.
It consists of coteries as well as encounters; in contrast with this
world, the 'Hôtel de la Mole' seems singularly monolithic.

Henry James accords a special status to the 'conscious beings' who
are formed, developed and come to 'realize themselves' through social
experience. In consequence one finds society both highly prized and
depreciated: prized because the consciousness of these 'special'
people is the focal point of their social relationships to which it was
possible, formerly, to refer only by invoking the novelist's 'omni-
science', and which are delineated by James with extraordinary
precision; depreciated, because James's heroes in the course of their
experience find social life increasingly discredited; for while it allows
them to become individual beings (in the strict sense of the term) it
reveals its true face as made up of trickery, meanness and constraint.
Life in society brings them proof that only the inner life is free,
liberating and authentic. Just as the scholar, after making a discovery
(one remembers Proust in the final pages of *Remembrance of Things
Past*), no longer concerns himself with the materials which led him
to it, so James's protagonists end by perceiving the facts of social
life as objects. The subject rejects the very thing that by its objectivity
makes his own subjectivity possible. This formula, intrinsic to
James's novels, is still more explicitly stated by Joyce, Virginia Woolf
and Musil. It is this which makes it possible for commentators
to overlook the extraordinary precision of the same writers' observations about the society of their time, and to make pronouncements
about their driving their heroes into an isolation that is gratuitous,

unreal, and easily labelled solipsist. In the same way, it becomes possible to suppose that, in choosing self rather than the world, these characters become more alienated than their acquaintances who, in their eyes, are non-sentient beings and who instead of developing their selves remain conventional dolls, thinking mostly of nothing but money. Any difference between Bloom and the Dubliners is only superficial while Swann's attitude to the 'Verdurin clique' demonstrates the importance of the myth of the ego for the bourgeois *Weltanschauung*. We have to recognize that for the narrator of *Remembrance of Things Past* social reality lacks both beauty and value. For him it is a matter of realizing himself as a work of art by exploring and coming to know the realm of his inner life. In James, too, there is one remarkable instance of sublimation: the rich American business man in *The Golden Bowl* who collects rare works of art in the hope that their market value can be transmuted into pure artistic value so that he himself can be identified with their beauty.

The more the novel emphasizes self-absorption to the detriment of connections with others, the more suspect the novelist becomes of being dominated by ideological structures which reflect the class system. There is good reason to wonder whether, in simply contemplating his inner life and in general regarding his own awareness as the only genuine value (and this is the case, to a certain extent, with the hero of *The Trial*), the fictional character is revealing the value judgements appropriate to a bourgeois conception of life, and is, in fact, attempting to resolve a 'crisis of values' – an idea which itself is rather artificial, being a device for bourgeois intellectuals to give themselves a clear conscience, and so is visibly an ideological weapon.

These questions become more acute when one finds the novelist deliberately cutting subjectivism off at the source so as to portray simply the externals of people and things and thus present the world as a phenomenon, pure and simple, without any circumstantial details. Robbe-Grillet's anti-subjectivism has been used as an excuse for calling him the impressario of a civilization dominated by technology, if not technocracy. Similarly, Nathalie Sarraute's 'infra-psychology' is used to give character to microcosms of sociability in which human relationships are dissected, so to speak, for entertainment. The novels of Henry Green (*Loving*)[3] and Chapman Mortimer (*A Stranger on the Stairs*)[4] in England and of Paul Bowles (*Let It Come Down*)[5] in the United States, can be interpreted in the same way, for here too the world is simply 'there', bereft of coherence or finality.

What is important to understand is that Robbe-Grillet is to Proust what Proust was to Tolstoy. Step by step the art of the novelist in the Western world has worked to erode personality and to slacken the bonds which it is possible to have with each other. Although he casts a veil of subjectivism over 'real' social relationships, Proust's novels always remain humanist. But in removing the veil, the so-called 'observer' school reveals that after a century of the market society, individuals and their relationships are no longer human. They have become things.

This process is not, of course, peculiar to the French novel. From the American – Salinger, Bellow and Burrows – to the young German novelists of today, all those writers who treat the novel or the short story as art have one fundamental theme in common: the impossibility of communication between persons. Put another way, they share a profoundly ironical view of the very concept of society.

It is, therefore, impossible not to return to concepts of class and class conflict for an explanation of the fact that after the decline of naturalism, Western novelists felt they had less and less right or ability to speak in the name of 'society'. The tendency has been for them to find value for the person first in his inner life and thereafter in his observing eye, and in nothing else. If one contrasts Balzac's sociological and historical perspective with the way in which Beckett dismembers the human being, humanism and humanity, there would be some truth in seeing this particular fate for the novel as a reflection of the progressive dissolution of society and of civilization into conflicting elements. And since it is the dominant class that bears responsibility for this dissolution, it is natural enough for these writers to come inevitably to be regarded as the accomplices of bourgeois ideology, having devoted so many pages to exploring the 'interstices of the heart', to descriptions of the 'view through the venetian blind' and even to attempts at reconciling the 'values' of civilization with the imperatives of revolutionary action. Nevertheless, the novel is a piece of work and to account for it as such one must have recourse to a more fundamental notion than that of class – the notion of production. For a sociologist (even for one who rejects Marxism) the novelist is a producer rather than a creator.

The idea of production applied to the arts, and especially to the novel, implies a paradox – which is, however, only a seeming paradox. The novelist can be seen as a producer in the very extent to which he is unaware of the actual modes of production in society – the forces which generate the class struggle. In fact, in writing his book the novelist inevitably becomes part and parcel of a system of ideological production which is designed to mask the real system of production, with all its antagonisms and conflicts.

The idea of production does manifestly provide a firm basis for the interpretation of the novel and even for assessing its artistic value. An interpretation on these lines has in the first place the advantage of showing clearly that the main conceptual framework of the writer, when he comes to compose fiction, is itself fictive. What he is dealing with is a collection of ideas, values, principles and theories which have seemingly some explanatory meaning for society as a whole and even the world itself, but which in reality derive from the subjective consciousness of one particular class. There is some justification for the idea that Proust and Thomas Mann looked at the social reality which they represented in their stories without really seeing it. However accurate their knowledge of that reality, they did not nevertheless cease to attribute to it a significance which they derived from the *Weltanschauung* of the social milieu in which they had been brought up. For example, the Narrator in *Remembrance of Things Past* watches with a deep sense of nostalgia the disintegration of the aristocracy as a caste, and the debasement of its values. For him the nobility represented a way of life with an aesthetic quality the bourgeoisie could only parody. Proust's sociological insights are for the most part worked out in terms of an ideal and of an idealistic frame of reference.

Nevertheless this Proustian sociology displays a truly scientific precision, which I believe is due primarily to the fact that he takes the 'fictive' ideology to which he refers his observations of social reality so seriously. These observations are accurate (they actually constitute a sociological document) because of the very fact that there is a truly appalling gap between the level of his own system of values, and that of the actual phenomena recollected from the experiences of his life. Any sociologist, Marxist or not, can distinguish the presence of factual contradictions – natural contradictions, one might say – between the values and the ideals which a social class uses as a form of protection, or which have a fascination for its members, and the objective social relationships which derive from the social relations of production which are themselves both real and conflict-ridden. The novelist, however, sees the contradiction between values and social existence only in terms of definition, or of degree.

It is in this difference between the two perceptions of the contradiction (a difference which Lukács discerned so profoundly) that the essential structure of the novel resides. For the novelist gives himself the primary – and impossible – task of establishing, through the mediacy of his hero, a coherent and credible relationship between a man's life and his reasons for living. As one of Malraux's characters says 'life is worth nothing, but nothing is worth life'. Nevertheless, the behaviour of the protagonists of *Man's Fate*, just like the behaviour of Melville's or Conrad's heroes, gives ample proof that life is impossible as soon as life stops making sense. So, one is confronted by a paradox: although the novel (at least as written by Cervantes, Tolstoy or Faulkner) is produced out of an ideology which is completely fictive, if not deceitful, it still gives us an accurate representation of a set of social relationships at one particular moment in history.

For purposes of analysis, it is necessary to see, as Lukács pointed out, how unbridgeable the gap is between the actual system of economic production and the 'system' of literary production, and to recognize that this gap gets ever wider from Balzac to Joyce. Yet it also has to be realized that the realistic novel would have been impossible without the 'interpretative delirium' which gripped Marivaux, Melville and Dostoyevsky when they applied themselves to the study of life and men. Faulkner would not have written his novels had he not seen the ancestral social order of the American South (which was in fact a class structure) perverted by all the groups which made up the South, and especially by the old families whose duty it was to sustain that order.

Nevertheless, Proust, Joyce and Faulkner have to admit defeat –

without necessarily recognizing it for what it is: their stories are a perpetual testimony to the power and the impotence of the ideologically determined fiction (which they took as reality) which governs the shape of their novels. The impotence of this ideology, its somehow hallucinatory nature, is made manifest at the end of the novel, an end which is death, even – perhaps especially – when the hero does not perish physically. Incapable of resolving the conflict between 'life' and its 'meaning' (a conflict which it is impossible to resolve 'objectively') the novelist obliterates it or, at the best, leaves it in suspense, like Proust, Joyce, Virginia Woolf. For the sociologist, values and ideals are alienating forces. For the writer and for his characters, they are forces which are inalienable and indefectible. Death is the only possible outcome for the hero of the novel, and his death carries with it a sociological lesson: a false problem can have no solution. The great novelist is one who is incapable either of lapsing into incredibility by equating living with reasons for living (even though that equation would justify his argument, and legitimate the behaviour of his hero) or of realizing that he has built his novel on the sands of 'ideas'.

Thus, in *Light in August*, the death of the pseudo-negro and pseudo-white, Christmas, at the end 'solves' – and consequently leaves intact – the conflict between the legendary 'South' and the fact of racism, the political and economic significance of which is fully recognized. This is not to say that Faulkner does not lay bare the forces at work in the South with superb sociological insight. At the same time, one needs to recognize that the social structure as it is portrayed by the writer amounts to a mode of expressing the essential value which he confers on life: Balzac's will to power, Dostoyevsky's grace, Robbe-Grillet's rejection of subjectivist and humanist illusions.

In every instance we see the novel not so much ending as *dissolving*, so as to put its governing theme, its central idea, in correct focus. This is manifest throughout, whether, as in Balzac, the final closure is represented by death, whether it is a Frédéric Moslan, whose end is implicit in Flaubert's well-known 'he travelled ... became acquainted with the melancholy world of passenger liners', but who has been extinguished forever by his own passive quality, whether it is Robbe-Grillet's *Voyeur* escaping the savage grip of

society, or whether it is the characters in *The Planetarium* revolving
ceaselessly around each other. Dissolution, in these various ways,
carries with it the demonstration that human problems cannot be
resolved within the class system. But it should also reveal to the
sociologist the fact that unless the writer sees values as of central
importance, the novel becomes impossible – at least in so far as
concerns its appropriateness for revealing to us how particular
social groups are constituted, and how they come to be in conflict, at
a particular time, and in a particular situation.

Literary analysis, it has been said, is a graveyard of structures.[6]
The logic of *Ulysses* or of *Man's Fate* is not a matter either of structure
or of structuralism. It is better to regard such novels as revealing the
social structure dominated by the middle classes for what it is: a
structure with a yawning cavity opening in it to receive its own
death.

The best example of this gaping structure is perhaps *The Magic
Mountain*. The novel is both product of and witness to a bourgeoisie
more and more given over to the profit motive, and so repudiating
the old liberal and humanist tradition. Thomas Mann portrays a well-
intentioned young man delivered from the materialistic and inhuman
influence of 'the people of the plain'. Taken away to live high up in
the mountains, in the enclosed and select setting of the sanatorium,
Castorp becomes the repository of conceptions of the world which
are contradictory but which, in the novelist's estimation, have
nevertheless to be reconciled. Only by bringing a liberal socialism
and violent revolutionary thought into some kind of harmony can
the world be saved from the inhumanity of capitalism and the havoc
of revolution. Then comes the outbreak of war. Mann's hero is
exposed to its full fury, but his destiny is not pursued further. Will
Castorp be killed, or will he survive, together with a culture, a
civilization capable of integrating all the aspects and aspirations of
humanity? By ending on this questioning note, all the more significant considering the book was written after 1918, the 'ideological
referent'[7] of Mann's novel is laid bare; it is the 'crisis of values', which
serves to conceal the real historical problems posed by class struggles.
Despite this, *The Magic Mountain* represents a significant contribution to the story of a particular civilization. In it we find an
exposé of the ideological complexity and of the variety of images of

society contained in the culture of the time. Novelists like Joyce, Mann, and Malraux practice a kind of imaginative sociology. They are able to grasp by empathy (mostly through emotional experience) what the sociologist or historian deals with in terms of facts or concepts.

The paradox of the novel, at least of those of Joyce or Proust, lies in the fact that these novelists are able to grasp facts in the raw – in concrete immediacy – although they have only been able to perceive their rawness and transmute them into literature by virtue of the ideological interpretation which they derive from their class position. But this paradox disappears as soon as one admits (and how can one not ?) that the novelist, while seeing and conveying this reality, surrenders himself to aesthetic considerations which I see as rectifying his dependence on the ideals and values proper to his cultural milieu and social origin. Moreover, there is also the fact that the further one moves away from the framework of the Balzac type of novel, the wider the gap between social reality and cultural reality, a gap which the great novelists are fully aware of.

The fact remains that *Ulysses*, to take one instance, testifies to the irreducibility of the opposition between the perception of what one might call 'living reality' and the indisputably abstract interpretation that the writer puts on it. Joyce was caught between two forces: on the one hand there was the weight of religious, moral and middle-class conventions which pressed down on Ireland, and on the other, the rebellion that was to free the people from that particular pressure. The writer chose to abandon both the latter and the former compulsion, and his voluntary exile might well be regarded as his brand of idealism. At all events, Joyce took it upon himself to reveal the concrete reality, the living everyday experience, of Dubliners (including Bloom and Daedalus) in a manner that comes close to surrealism. All through *Ulysses* people and things seem to be emerging from their carapace of ideology as the writer shatters it. They make their appearance 'existentially', taking the word in its Sartrian sense. But Joyce executes this exposure only in terms of a single conception of value: the inner life of consciousness, embodied and acted out by Bloom and by Stephen Daedalus. And this particular value can be regarded as revealing complicity with the bourgeois idealism oppressing Ireland rather than with the struggle of the Irish rebellion. The stream of consciousness, which is the main fabric of Joyce's novel and which conveys its meaning, is thus open to two sociological interpretations: Joyce could be regarded as recreating humane culture out of its religious and bourgeois ashes (for he shows us that every aspect of the world, even the most trivial, is in itself poetic once it is liberated from the oppression of conventions and 'culture'); or one might consider that *Ulysses*, in which the poetry of everyday life is revealed, erects one more screen to obscure reality and the necessity of class struggle by his revelation of the poetry of existence, since Joyce is content to turn the real forces of oppression – the Church and the State – into abstractions, as he in fact does.

Clearly, we are now dealing with two kinds of sociology of the novel. One sees the great Western novelists as revealing what is lacking to make society truly human or social; the other is concerned with establishing the fact that in revealing what is lacking (and this is as plain in Joyce as it is in Proust; to survive, one only has to grasp the 'poetry of life and of objects') the writer is only rendering an account of the state of society – of the class structure in which he himself remains imprisoned. This interpretation would not call for any amendment if it accounted for the techniques which made it possible for Joyce, for example, to deal sociologically with one of the largest human collectivities contained within the novel.

The same holds true in the case of Kafka's work. The bank clerk in *The Trial* and his relationships with other people are undeniably realistic and valid in a historical sense; they belong to the Prague of 1910. Starting from the vividness of this actual situation, the sociologist can either take Kafka's novel at face value or regard it as a cultural product determined by ideological contradictions of peculiar complexity.

According to the first view, Kafka's hero is engaged in a legitimate but symbolic rebellion. His revolt, in fact, signifies the confrontation between an individual and the State – a confrontation in which society plays no mediating part. Society can be said to be neutral, if one takes neutrality to mean tacit conformity with the established order set up by political power. 'K's' first mistake is in believing that a humane, just, enlightened and intelligent society is able to intervene between him, as a single individual, and the State. This reaction, founded upon a misconception, is transformed by authority into a crime; for the administration of the Austro-Hungarian Empire forbids its citizens, especially Jews, to entertain any desire to 'comprehend' the authority of the State, beyond certain limits. In betraying his impatience 'K' is guilty of not admitting that the administrative apparatus can contradict the human values which it is supposed to represent and to promote in the way it performs its functions. From this point of view (which I shall develop later), Kafka's novel seems to be a remarkable critical analysis of the liberal state.

If we follow the second interpretation, *The Trial* demonstrates what a class system, decked out with all the ideological attributes of order and justice, can do to the individual. Perhaps we ought indeed to 'burn Kafka'. Impotent and downtrodden to such an extent that he cannot envisage any outcome other than death (or resignation, which comes to the same thing) the hero of *The Trial* is the archetypal non-revolutionary. He is capable of nothing because capitalist society has lured him into a nothingness which fascinates him.

Robbe-Grillet's novels can be seen to contain evidence of a similar dual significance. The historical reality of their contents is indisputable. But granted this realism, do we really have to believe that, the world being what it is, *Le Voyeur* shows us where the only possible kind of autonomy (the visual) is to be found (as the writer himself says in his critical works)? Or, as against this, is one to think of Robbe-Grillet's characters as typifying the passivity which characterizes men at a certain stage of economic capitalism?[8]

It can be argued that the great realistic novelists betrayed the ideological framework to which their work was fundamentally tied – provided the word 'betray' is read in both senses: to reveal and to repudiate. In fact their work revealed, first, that a 'world vision' is really a vision which is partisan and applicable only to part of reality; secondly, that the society which the writer believes himself to experience directly is really seen by him through a glass distorted by bourgeois culture. But the same work repudiates its own overall intention both through the death which awaits the hero and, more especially, because of the real substance of the novel, which, whatever the author makes of it, reveals the existence of insoluble contradictions, in the Marxist sense. Thus reality outdoes fiction, although it must be emphasized that this is in itself the product of art and not of technique and artifice.

Translation – betrayal: this is the ambiguity in the novel on which 'interpretations' of the novel are based – interpretations which we shall subsume under the terms of the general theory of fictional production. The theory originates with Georg Lukács, whose work on literary fiction has inspired some outstanding research, in particular that of Lucien Goldmann. Lukács related the significance of the novel to the two polarities between which society exists – one being its myths, the other the realities of interpersonal relationships. By this means he exposed, from 1915 onwards, the inadequacy of literary historicism and positivist sociology. *The Theory of the Novel* showed that writing fiction is essentially a matter of trying to reconcile actual social relationships, which are determined by the infrastructure of production, with the ideals or values which the individual hopes to realize in his own life and which are already inscribed in myths. This reconciliation is impossible. It is in this impossibility that *Don Quixote*, or *Anna Karenina* find their origin and their achievement.

As we shall see in the following chapter, which is concerned with the relationship between myth and the novel, Lukács penetrated the fundamental significance of the part played by fiction in Western civilization. But 'significance' is meaningless without there being something to be significant about. Whether he is dealing with European realism, the historical novel, or the meaning of 'critical realism', Lukács is concerned unremittingly with the problems of form. The novel is not a reflection of the myriad aspects of social intercourse; it is, on the contrary, the mirror itself.

A theory based on the concept of production must nevertheless take account of the artistic structure of the novel. It is obvious that, as Henry James has emphasized, 'form alone preserves and sustains content'.[9] But a sociologist, especially a Marxist, can hardly take a writer at his word when he claims – often to defend himself from a charge of standing for 'art for art's sake' – that there cannot be content without form. The form of the novel has to be understood as meaning not only the style of the writing but also the manner in which it is constructed. Moreover, when James says that form and content are indissociable, he is speaking as artist just as much as observer and interpreter of social reality. Most theoretical writings by novelists tend to emphasize the necessity of a dialectical relationship between facts as observed, experienced and thought, and their formal representation. Yet these same writers seldom fail to claim autonomy for their own work in relation to reality. At one level, the novel is a product of conscious mental effort; at another level, an artistic creation. Anyone who accepts the production theory of the novel, or of literature in general, finds these two forms of creative action already present at the level of observed historical and social reality, or rather, that this latter presents the writer with the basic materials on which he works through those two forms of action. What the novelist sets to work on is, first, a particular set of actual social relationships and, secondly, a particular set of ideological conditions which apply to those relationships. His talent, or genius, lies in his ability to transcribe what is already, for him, inscribed in reality: but this transcription is entirely his own affair, and the fact that he is unaware of these fundamental pre-conditions poses a crucial problem. The structure of any novel in its most clearly artistic aspects is authored, in the first place, by social psychological and ideological factors, to the existence of which the writer himself testifies. The writer does not impose form. He reveals it.

Revelation is accomplished through the medium of processes of thought which involve the writer although they are not 'personal' to him: they go to make his image of the world (*Weltanschauung*). Neither Lukács nor his followers thought of the completed novel as being something separable from the objective conditions of its production. The concept of image of the world allowed them to bring to light a logical relationship between these two aspects of the novel or of drama.

The images of the world present in the work of Racine, or Pascal, or Dostoyevsky, or Kierkegaard arise in the first place from their realization of the relationsips actually prevailing in society being irreconcilable with the ideas and values to which they, as writers or philosophers, are attached. Life, in their eyes, is made up of insoluble conflicts. Yet this view of reality does not make them inclined to question their own system of values. On the contrary, for them the split is not between the concrete and the abstract but between contingent facts and universal ideas – hence the importance of the idea of renunciation, which dominates the work of Pascal and the other three writers, and is also to be found in all the great novels (at least until the 1950s – Beckett's characters are isolated, not abandoned). Thus, while, in *The Possessed*, man is foresaken in a religious sense – the supreme gift of grace is at once offered and withdrawn by God – in Balzac's novels man's salvation depends on whether or not he is aware of belonging to some social apparatus. In *La Comédie humaine* the very concept of society is to Vautrin what the idea of salvation is to Stavrogin. When we come to the world of Proust, what can be said is that it is one which has been foresaken by artistic consciousness, a species of awareness which only the narrator fully possesses, and which implies the deepest and most extensive self-awareness.

The structure of tragedy in Racine as revealed by Goldmann in *The Hidden God*[10] can also be found in the novels of Faulkner. In both the central figure is a cruel and jealous god, pitiless and indifferent to human life. The divine presence, withdrawn from humanity, forces the individual to try to achieve his own salvation, although this endeavour is, from the start, utterly useless. The triangle made up of God (indifferent), sin (original) and salvation (impossible), can be found in both *Phèdre* and *Light in August*. Yet it has none of the universal reality and significance which Racine and Faulkner seem to attribute to it. This metaphysical formula does not constitute the nature of man which, because it has become perverted, degrades all human relationships, but a conception of the life of man which has been forged by one social class in order to put down other classes.

Hence the originality of the writer lies first of all in his acute awareness of an unbridgeable gulf of unmeaning between a universal idea of man and the contingent social reality which he sees around him. The writer conceives his work in terms of this discovery, of which he is made aware by reality, or rather, by history. After the discovery of what we have called irreconcilability, the perception of it enters into the writer's conception of his heroes and his secondary characters. The heroes are victims of the split between the ideal and reality. They are consumed by the desire not only to know the cause of their torment but also to end it by devoting their energies to reconstructing these two apparently irreconcilable domains, or levels of existence, into some harmonious whole. As against this, the secondary characters are conformists. They are integrated into a contingent social world from which they profit, or to which they submit without a word. Emma Bovary as against Homais, Anna Karenina as against her husband (and her lover) and Leopold Bloom as against the Dubliners, all belong to this pattern. The central concern is in every case with beings who are doomed, Hamlet-like, by their conscience, while others are either saved or crushed by their lack of conscience. It is only today that one no longer finds at the centre of the novel a hero torn between the spectacle of life as it is and the vision of the world as it should be.

But although the hero of the novel is a victim of a variety of conflicts and contradictions, these same contradictions are envisaged by the novelist as an ordered pattern. Reality seems to be spread out before him with all its conflicting forces – of black and of white in Faulkner – which the writer is then able to synthesize in his work by setting them out in the terms, and through the means, of some basic ideological principle. This pattern is the world vision achieved by the writer, the first real stage of the work yet to be written.

This analysis of the concept of world vision does not, I think, differ substantially from Goldmann's definition: there is first 'the conceptual extrapolation of the actual, effective and intellectual tendencies of the group to its ultimate coherent form' and, secondly, a 'coherent set of problems and responses which expresses, in creative literature, a concrete world of people and things through the medium of words'.[11] The hero of the novel may not realize the unity between the ideal world and his actual life, but the completeness of the world of the novel as a whole can be realized – the novel can become an artistic totality – because the writer has perceived social reality, at all its different levels, as the arena for a struggle that he does not define as a class struggle. For Tolstoy and Faulkner, reality is made up of people and groups tearing themselves to pieces through ignorance of the values which might save and unite them.

In the light of the concepts of world-vision and of production, Faulkner's 'South' appears to be an organism made up of many conflicting elements which are yet indissociable from each other.

This organism is translated into the plot and the complex world of *Absalom, Absalom*. Faulkner's 'South' owes its existence to – is made real and visible in – the aesthetic character of the book in so far as the novel itself has been determined, though not caused, by a previous form of actual production composed out of a social and ideological ordering.

If we take a different view, and regard Faulkner as the inventor of forms which do not exist in real life, we have inevitably to treat the work of art as a frame which encases some material chunk of reality, which means shifting from the novel as 'pure' form, as an explanatory concept for fiction, to the humble and rather banal sociological idea of content. If the novel is studied in terms of production as a fundamental concept, it becomes easier to demonstrate its artistic nature than is possible by analysis in aesthetic terms alone, because it becomes possible to demonstrate the historical and social necessity of forms of fiction.

Form as product or form as producer?

We have presented some of the arguments with which the theory of literary production can confront literary history and, especially, literary criticism. The question, however, is whether study based on the idea of production can *conserve* the aesthetic quality of the novel in its guise as a social fact – whether this applies to the work itself or to the effect produced by its forms on a society and its culture. Admittedly, the sociology of the novel has not yet achieved studies of the level attained by Panofsky and Francastel in their work on the plastic arts. Although there are any number of studies which set out to interpret society through its literature, there are few which help one to read society and its history in the novel itself, treated as a work of art (and even the most stereotyped sentimental novel is still a creative work). Regrettably, too much research disregards the fact that a world-vision is as closely attached to a particular form as a sign is to what it signifies – which is not in the least to be taken to mean that a work of art is simply a sign. Just as Panofsky has shed

light on the specific relationship between the Gothic arch and
scholastic thought, so it would be feasible to relate the linguistic
currency of fiction in a particular period to the actual language
content thought appropriate in the same historical period. The
example of Francastel, who examines the progressive destruction by
modern art of the plastic space elaborated from the Renaissance
onwards, can also be usefully applied to literature. We have seen
the destruction of the social territory we recognize as Balzac's and,
later Proust's and Joyce's, although many novelists today try to
revive these social territories (very often by mixing them up).
Considerable importance, therefore, attaches to the work of Erich
Auerbach. *Mimesis* presents excerpts, from Homer to Virginia Woolf,
of imaginative literature and shows how these texts, through their
style and organization, and above all by the position adopted by the
narrator (sometimes as the omniscient author, sometimes hiding
behind people and things) delineate the successive modes of social
and cultural relationships in the development of Western civilization.[12]

Today, however, especially in France, there are two approaches to
fiction that emphasize the necessary and coherent bond between
literary and social forms. The work of Lukács and his followers,
deriving from Marxist thought,[13] can be set against the research of
the Russian formalists of the 1930s and also compared with the
methods and findings of the linguistic structuralists.[14] It is when they
examine the meanings of actual narration that the historically-
minded and the structuralists most frequently come to blows. The
theory of fictional production is explicitly sociological. Formalism
(which is by no means wholly opposed to dialectical materialism)
is only indirectly or implicitly sociological. The work of the formalists cannot be ignored in a sociological study of narrative since they
are concerned with language as a basic social phenomenon (rendered
into written form so far as literature is concerned, although it is the
transition from language forms as used in social interaction to
narrative forms that is the central concern in the work of formalists).
Yet the meaning that the formalists find within (not underneath)
these forms must be to a large extent sociological. By announcing
as the first princple of their critical method the grasp of the text
itself exclusive of reference to anything outside it, the Russian

formalists present humane studies and the social sciences with one totally isolated object as the material of scholarly investigation, which, by their very nature and methods, they hesitate to treat in this way – as something written.

Yet, formalists and structuralists, in denying that literature can ever, strictly speaking, be a *social* object, nevertheless treat the concept of production as relevant. According to the Marxist, and, more generally, the sociological, concept of literary work, fiction is as much a matter of production as it is of revelation, in the sense of being already 'structured' or 'constructed'. Only one thing is missing from this complex social and ideological relationship which is the object of this kind of approach, and that is the element which actually signifies the presence of everything else: the completed work.

Formalism does regard fiction in production terms, but more in the sense of being an energizer, with its significance 'formed' in the matrix of reality with the same kind of connotation as attaches to words and to systems of words which are similarly formulated out of actual circumstance. Just as Saussure established a radical difference between '*parole*' and '*langage*', formalism, I believe, distinguishes spoken (or rather 'living') language from literary writing while insisting (and this is their main point) on the complementarity of the two.

Let me try to make this more clear. In the case of formalism, living language makes do without literature, even though literature has living language implicit within it, and even explains or explicates it. The formalist school regards our social relationships, our myths, our ideologies as having no reality other than what obtains in a language or in everyday speech, which is the everyday medium of expression for these relationships, myths and ideologies. In this context, reality *is* meaning. Yet in everyday experience, such meaning lies at the implicit level; we make use of it, one way or another, without stopping to think about it. This is where literature comes in, since it *unveils* meaning and, therefore, the world of actuality. The act of telling a story (in the widest sense of the term, for both history and philosophy are also literature) can extract from the language of everyday use its hidden meaning, and hence the actual objects to which it refers, whether these be events, ideas or feelings. Literature expresses and brings to life the living content of words.

One can take the description of the Pension Vauquer in *Le Père Goriot* and interpret it in terms of 'production' or in terms of the formalist perspective. Considered as both production and as revelation, Balzac's text offers us a social reality conceived by a determinist, positivist and historical mode of thought, by which men are represented by the objects they look at or possess (even if possession only means paying the price of their board in a pension) or which surround them. These men and these things are distanced from each other necessarily and indefeasibly by use-value, which really means exchange value. At the other end of the scale, one might say, Robbe-Grillet tells us that men are no longer represented by things – they *are* things, exchange value having replaced use-value so completely as to absorb people, who are thus identified with exchange value, without actually being aware of it. In *Père Goriot* the individual is his context; in *Le Voyeur* the context is the man, who therefore has no longer any individuality. The fictional Pension Vauquer reveals a real Pension Vauquer – a crossroads of interests and classes, an intermediate term (as Madame Vague is herself 'intermediate') between Goriot's downfall, Vautrin's calculated dissembling (who is the 'dangerous' type of person[15] able to move from one class to another, for we have already reached a time when the full effects of social mobility – the mobility obtainable by money – are discernible) and the manoeuvres of Rastignac who, although he 'has' class, no longer bears its insignia – money.

According to the formalists, the description of the Pension Vauquer should produce, generate, a depressing wretched place, just as words produce things. Actually, any such product is something which remains unperceived by Vautrin, Rastignac or Goriot because they 'say things' for entirely 'subjective' reasons, and in so doing they make things 'nothings'. In ordinary life, speech slides over objects, our language exists in our consciousness only within the framework of our intentions, of all that we want out of life; it exists unconsciously when it comes to the 'immediate' content of the words we are using as signs. But in the world of the novel, a system of signs (the attributes of the *Pension Vauquer*) constructs, sentence after sentence, characters (who are not even there) by presenting what is concealed within their language. It is this concealed aspect that is essentially social, for the words used by the writer, and the way in which he deploys them, relates directly to objects in all the solidity of their very existence. Literature can engender reality because it takes on the *role* rather than the function of language, a role which consists in designating things. In ordinary life, we use language only unthinkingly as a matter-of-course affair. Literature makes what is implicit in language explicit. It is also text, and text as production; the novelist, whatever his experience or his talent, faces reality as what lies in front of him, not in what has been completed. He must work at it and work incessantly, weaving every thread for the reader to follow. It is this work of his that constitutes the reality of which the reader is conscious; it is the *written* words (and not just speech, images or thoughts) that designate and construct reality for the reader. The writing of a novel and its subsequent reading are fundamentally social acts which complement each other, since they turn into shape, into order, into something evident, our primordial mode of social activity which yet remains for the most part unacknowledged: the spoken word.

The study of literary work '*qua* literature' does not consist in peeling off a surface of pure forms so as to uncover other layers of meaning underneath.* Formalism does not lay bare a story as some arbitrary, spontaneous creation, uninfluenced by all the historical and social facts which, as all the evidence shows, provide the material for the writer to work on. On the contrary, the social facts existing in literature can only be shown to be an integral part of it if they are read in the very fabric of the narrative itself, and not 'between the lines'.

James's famous *Figure in the Carpet* can be taken to symbolize the formalist conception of literature; the content of the story is like the

---

*We may be criticized for applying the identical term 'formalist' to students whose work follows the line of a Russian formalist like V. Propp (translated into French as *Morphologie du conte*, Paris, 1970) and also to those (notably, the contributors to *Tel Quel*) who, far from limiting themselves to the study of the 'rhetoric' or the 'poetics' of a work of fiction, uncover in its language two kinds of structure – the socio-economic structure of Marx's analysis, and the unconscious structuring of Freud's. The only point of the contrast made here between the 'formalist school' and the 'production school' is to establish the distinction between those for whom 'the formal' represents a starting point and those who regard it as a culmination to be achieved.

'secret' of a writer's art. It is pointless to look for this 'secret' in the writer's personality; it is inscribed only in his text.

The theories or methods which I have tried to outline have already put a stop to the damage done by the long tradition of historicist and, especially, impressionistic criticism. The first school shows that the form of the novel always derives its meaning from the social. The second regards meaning as contained entirely within the words on the page. Both the sociological and the formalist schools of thought have restored to fiction its full integrity as an organic and organized whole. The Russian formalists considered literature *qua* literature and the novel (as a specific work) was also regarded in this way by Lukács. Yet between these two fundamentally original theories of literature; one has to find a place for Forster's important *Aspects of the Novel*, as the first really structural, or at least thematic, analysis of fiction in its entirety.

Significance or meaning?

To borrow an expression of Foucault's, the novel today has ceased to be a monument and has become a document.[16] Significant of (or rather, signifying) a particular historico-social situation, the novel seems to be 'written into' reality, instead of appearing to be some kind of miraculous phenomenon. From the most banal detective stories to *La Maison de rendezvous*, the novel remains an artistic fact and *therefore* a social fact. The sociologist is perhaps too much inclined to be satisfied with working out the significant relationship of a particular novel (which is above all *innovative*) to a particular socio-historico-ideological complex – a complex in which the nerve-centre is the writer's position in the class system. On the other hand there is the danger of formalism's clinging too closely to linguistic structuralism, dwelling on the disclosure of the rhetoric, the language of discourse, of a story as structures signifying some intrinsic reality. Again, when the sociologist examines and arranges the elements of the content of a novel, they may reveal themselves as simply a collection of data actually related to language itself, and not to the reality of the social system.

Those who adopt this formalist viewpoint will doubtless remark on the inadequacy of a theory of production according to which 'everything has one meaning', and which asserts that the components (even the artistic elements) of every single work are 'given', contained in history, even before it is written. Once it has been worked out, once it has become a work of art, all the novel can explain is what explains it; its unique meaning is assimilated into the meaning of its origin. Malraux's novel, for example, originates in a crisis of Western civilization and of its system of values, a crisis which the group of intellectuals engaged in the revolutionary struggle are trying to resolve. Yet this struggle, by its very nature, negates these values, or is at any rate alien to them. In its entirety as much as in each of its elements – characters, dialogue and descriptions – *La Condition humaine* gives form to an impossible compromise between the need to bring about the revolution and the need to remain faithful to an old civilization, primarily to its aesthetic values.[17] For the formalist, such an account of Malraux's novel neglects its essential quality, which is that of a structured discourse which is the vehicle of a series of human relationships, which are real only so far as they are uttered in words. It is in fact on the very quality of that structured discourse that the influence of *La Condition humaine* is based, as well as its reputation as a literary achievement. A sociology of art based on the concept of world-vision and identifying this concept with the surface reality of a particular form betrays the kind of defective eyesight which Freud reveals in his study of Jensen's *Gradiva*. Freud's analysis tends to present this story as revealing some psychological process rather than explaining its form, and, consequently, its meaning. It is pointless, in a formalist interpretation of narrative, to move beyond the domain of the language used, which is what conveys the world-visions of writers in clear and precise terms.

For those, however, who regard the novel as a system of signs (in the wide sense of the term), its true qualities and sociological meaning are seen to be part of the science of signs, semiology, developed by Saussure. Confronting sociologists with the discoveries of linguistics, the formalist can accuse them of moving straight from the sign (the novel) to a series of references – (world vision, social relationships) – without taking account of the signifier or of what is signified. Between the work of the school of formalism and that of Lukács and his followers, the difference is one which separates *meaning* from *significance*. The meanings of constructed discourse as construed by formalists (Barthes, for instance, on the drama of Racine) are defined by them as facts. But for Marxist sociology factual reality is something signified *by* the written work.

The virtue of Freudian commentaries on literature, however, as well as Goldmann's conception of the sociology of the novel, is that aesthetic forms are related to a reality that is already composed. Whether explanation is in terms of the unconscious or of ideology, the writer in either case is regarded as being presented with reality in terms of a significant whole, or possibly a representation of some reality other than itself. The theory of the novel as product rejects formalism on the grounds that if the work of art articulates or aggregates or synthesizes or organizes concepts of production, of conflict, of class struggle and of world-vision, these concepts are themselves realities which transcend the work itself and which must be related to it, if what is signified by the 'Verdurin clique', the confrontation of Nephta and Settembrini in *The Magic Mountain*, and the death of Kyo and Kataw in *La Condition humaine*, is really to be understood. Formalism by itself cannot provide the key to aspects of the novel such as these.

The two modes of interpretation which I have discussed (and on which I have, of course, put my own interpretation) re-introduce the novel to social reality without, however, identifying it with that reality. There is no sense in which studies based on dialectical materialism represent the novel as a looking-glass. Nor do studies which derive from structural linguistics regard it as an artistic creation detached from reality. Whether fiction is dependent on society, or is independent of it, is not a problem of fact but of method. When it is (as so often nowadays) a matter of deciphering literature in terms of a product, with its own special meaning or significance, the method used involves determining the degree of consciousness existing in the writer first as observer of social reality and secondly as presenting it. Implicitly or explicitly, traditional literary history raises no question about either the writer's clear-sightedness or his independence. He is regarded as fully aware of the facts and the factors out of which his work is born and of the procedures and conventions his writing follows, and accepted as some extraordinary individual who is in undisputed command of reality. By contrast, contemporary work on literature, which is becoming more and more 'scientific', tends to demystify the personality of the creative author. Perhaps, however, such research is merely replacing the imaginary figure of the omniscient author with the equally extravagant image of the writer completely lacking in consciousness. Such studies go too far in crediting the writer with no sociological insight whatsoever; he has to be utterly ignorant about the actual process of social relationships, and this ignorance becomes the source of ambiguities and contradictions, which somehow need to be deciphered in order to discover the 'real' significance of the novel.

The notion of code appears to play an essential role in the work of the formalist school. More precisely, formalism distinguishes, in a single narrative, several different coding levels, of which the first is the language out of which the writer constructs what is narrated. One need not regard reasoning couched in terms of 'life' or 'freedom' as incompatible with reasoning concerned with 'system' or 'structure'. Both regard fiction, correctly, as a concord of signs emerging in essentially the form of imaginative literature. One of the most valuable contributions of formalism is (or could be) the application to these works of an explanatory method derived from their very composition. Criticism, as Heidegger has suggested, resembles (or should resemble) those woodland paths which 'lead nowhere', since they are a natural part of the woods they wander about in.[18] Formalism is also entirely justified in claiming that, in principle, the writer is to literature what the individual novelist is to fiction in general and what we are to our language. Speaking a language means that the language speaks *through* us. There is, however, a danger that formalism may reduce the existence of the facts as represented through constructed discourse to the level of modalities of such discourse, thereby reducing the actual narrative to the methods used to account for it. It is true enough that every science creates its own subject; but need it go so far, becoming to all appearances, indistinguishable from it?[19]

Formal code and social code

The linguist does not have to bother with subject matter, but only with the relationship between it and an apparatus of language, when he demonstrates just how this apparatus refers to subjects rather than representing them. If we attempted a commentary on the opening of *Père Goriot* following the formalist approach, we should want to emphasize that the specific and unique role of literature is to bring the reader to an awareness of the *artificiality* of language, in order to make him perceive reality exactly as it is. Writing should reveal the discreteness of words and things, so that the latter is seen to be contingent and thus to express one aspect of social reality: the context necessary for human action. Ordinary language involves objects in so far as they are used and useful; literature consists in a process of designating objects as existing. Here we should note a paradox which threatens to devalue critical analysis based on the structural nature of language. Too whole-hearted a commitment to the linguistic method may lead one to forget that the attitude of the writer as observer and then translator of reality is close to that of the linguist, for he must keep his mind equally separate from things as from words. The writer is, in fact, conscious of a tension, even perhaps – at the very extreme – of a contradiction, between the experience he has lived through and the reality of language as system and artifact. It is those writers for whom literature seems to be an absurdity who express reality in the most concrete and critical terms. But before resolving this contradiction by his writing, the author has already behaved as a linguist during the life he has lived hitherto. How could he realize how wide the gap is between speech as it is understood and the things, facts, intentions and social relationships underlying speech, other than by adopting the role of linguist? As James suggested, in *The Art of Fiction*, the 'real' is what fate must reveal, sooner or later, for us to know. Fiction, on the other hand, consists in what can never be brought to our knowledge except through 'splendidly wandering' thoughts and desires. Past experience is accepted language; the understanding of experience is a language which has been analysed, dissected and interpreted. It must also be realized that the originality of a novelist, or his lack of it, is assessed in terms of the importance he attaches to the search.

What I am suggesting is that the social and psychological elements to be found in a novel derive exclusively from speech as the writer has developed it for his own purposes, but that the reality and truthfulness of this speech are not limited to its forms. Truthfulness and reality lie in *what* he designates as, or in, objects, and not in *how* he presents them. Formalist and structuralist interpretations have perhaps unwittingly made a remarkable contribution to the sociology of literature by revealing literary activity as condition, not consequence, of reality. It is, however, hard to believe that an analysis or commentary on a text can dissect or reconstruct narrative speech without following it, i.e., without clarifying its subject, which is some kind of revelation. By taking one's bearings from the characteristic mode of speech of the novel and the linguistic elements it comprises the constituent factors are revealed of a reality which, in its turn, is relevant to sociology proper.

From this point of view, we can attempt the examination of certain aspects of Proust's work. This is in no sense an attempt to reconcile the two methods, but rather to show how they can illuminate one another.

The world of *Remembrance of Things Past* is defined by its diction, its '*logos*', much more clearly than Balzac's or Stendhal's. The social subject matter with which Proust had to deal was composed of people whose mode of speech, of necessity, placed them (as most of them were well aware) in the special enclave of 'Society'. This mode of speech serves both to express their social situation (or the situation to which they aspired) and to mask their real purposes. The remarks of the cook at Combray contain a whole sociology of the servants' quarters in one section of the bourgeoisie. Françoise's verbal dominance bespeaks the relative autonomy and familiarity of servants belonging to a family which they respect and which, in turn, respects them. To take another instance, the expression '*faire cattleyas*', used by Swann when he wants to caress Odette de Crécy, has a sociological rather than psychological meaning. The *cattleyas* express the gulf between the demi-mondaine and the man of quality who, given his origins, would not have had access to Society without the distinction, brilliance and originality of his language. Swann's *cattleyas* conveys to the reader how interconnected his social alienation and his psychological alienation are. For, in speaking to Odette in the mode of speech he uses to amuse the Guermantes, Swann is seeking to 'poeticize' his desire for a woman who is an 'unsuitable' attachment for him, but who would nevertheless be suitable, if only he dare obey the demands of purely sexual desires. But such daring is impossible for him, and not merely because he has a 'psychological' need to be unhappy; his courage fails him before Odette also because she asks to be treated cynically, in terms of power, and money, not in terms of *cattleyas* – these 'socialite' flowers bear witness to Swann's psychic masochism. As the novel continues, it appears that the only *cattleyas* acceptable to Odette are those of marriage, a marriage through which Swann is punished for having been truly poetic, truly civilized, in a world of completely artificial refinement. Although the *cattleyas* help Swann to enter the respectable world it is through his legitimate though scandalous union (masochists often being prepared to take desperate risks) that he is able to establish himself in a social class into which he is eventually integrated through a process almost Balzacian in its determinism.

Implicit in the language of the faithful servant, Françoise, and of the fortunate aesthete, Swann, is the class system, together with all its contradictions. Yet how is it this sociological reality is revealed to the reader in a kind of writing that is so completely different from Balzac's – as different as seeing a drawing of something is from actually seeing the object itself? Product and observer of a world where people prefer to express themselves in metaphorical language – although the metaphors themselves are formulae – the writer catches them and their language in their own trap: 'beauty'. Françoise, Bloch and Saint-Loup compose in their words a kind of poetry out of the factual elements of their situation – social class, occupation, money, desire, culture. The pictures of the different worlds in *Remembrance of Things Past* are drawn with that characteristic verbal brilliance which comprehends a complex range of appetites and frustrations. From a world that either affects, or is affected by, beauty and graciousness, Proust extracts an art, a

technique of language. The worldly aestheticism, to which he sub-
scribed in his early writing, written to please 'Monsieur de Norpois',
became transformed aesthetically. By betraying (both revealing and
being traitor to) those whom he observes, Proust is able to reproduce,
through a system of metaphor and metonymy, a complex social
system in which is spoken a kind of language which serves as a code.[20]
The members of this society endeavour to wrap the actuality of
things, desires and interests in verbal gauze, through which others
have to grasp all the nuances. The rhetoric of Proust's language of
discourse (images, sequence of phrases, arrangement of sections of
narrative) reconstitutes the organic reality of a social order which
seeks to conceal the fact that it is made of flesh and blood. Its
imagery, far from transfiguring reality, intensifies it, deepens it and
thus enables the reader to perceive and feel things almost in 'flesh
and blood' terms. Yet the writer does not in any sense change the
'use value' of objects into 'subjective value'. Their function as social
signifiers remains at the centre of metaphor which, like a magnifying
glass, gives an enlarged view of reality. In Proust's style of writing
a water jet at the Guermantes' becomes a fountain; an ornament
appropriate to a particular social class.

What must be understood before the specifically sociological meaning of Proust's novel becomes apparent is the clear distinction which
obtains between language as an artistic medium and language itself
– or rather, the 'self-same' language of the world the writer knows. In
literature, words which are ordinarily objects become signs of
existential realities. Proust's artistic code, which is made up of
metaphors, can only be decoded into metaphoric formulae – into
stereotypes and customary forms of language which themselves
represent a social code, and hence social structures and relationships.
Central to Proust's art is the strength and weakness of speech, as
Dr Cottard demonstrates by clothing his personality in elaborate
word-play for as long as he is unsure of his social status but, as soon as
he becomes Professor Cottard, abandoning all his verbal mannerisms.
Altogether, the rhetoric of *Remembrance of Things Past* contains a
significant hierarchy of characters; at the top stands the Narrator,
and immediately below him Swann and Charlus are the only
characters aware of the latent power of language in concealing or
desiring or betraying it. Yet this very awareness gives them away,

for instead of resorting like 'the others' to the formulae that enable Cottard, Forcheville and the Verdurins to achieve their ends without appearing to be trying, Swann and Charlus, the narrator's two doubles, use language in an original and aesthetic manner thinking that by doing so, they can get what they want and at the same time disguise the fact. It is through this 'aesthetic' language that they become traitors to their social milieu, in which they are tolerated without being admitted to membership, and where everyone is on the lookout for every false move they make. Swann and Charlus are in fact 'Narrators' who will not, or cannot, understand (because they lack the Narrator's 'talent') that it is only by constructing a work of art, not by aestheticizing life, that they can be spared the suffering that their perceptiveness inflicts on them – or at least compensate them for it or redeem them. The Narrator himself endures the same rebuffs as Swann and Charlus, but he is able to heal the wound made by the constant misunderstanding which exists between himself and society by creating a work of art whose forms (style, technique) become the 'optical instrument' by means of which social facts are revealed and denounced – facts that have continually wounded his thoughts and his feelings. Proust is one of the writers best able to show us the solitariness of the artist in terms of its sociological necessity. His solitude is a social product which reproduces social life – not something alienated from it. Yet Balzac's 'non-solitude', too, was something defined in terms of production, derived from the language of discourse of a society.

If, however, *Remembrance of Things Past* is itself made up of a set of codes, which have to be decoded, they are not reducible merely to the rules that govern the language of discourse. Proust, as he himself has shown, was looking for the overriding rules governing his own consciousness as well as the complex social milieux which he was describing. The elaboration of Proust's system goes far beyond that of literary rhetoric, which, as we have tried to show, derives from a transfer process from actual language as its exists in everyday life. Proust, moreover, has also managed to integrate into his work the resuls of his inner experience and of a social reality that he has correctly deciphered. He has realized that both are systems, organic wholes, despite their surface incoherence.

Again, the code we find inscribed in *Remembrance of Things Past* may itself be regarded as a set of psychological and social facts from which the writer has extracted 'laws'. It is by rationalizing his past experience in this way that the writer is able to deduce the working methods which he spells out for us, as most of the great writers have done in their theoretical writings on the novel. The idea of a code does indeed enable one to conceive of the existence, as a sociological fact, of the interior monologue, if one takes this to mean not so much a strictly personal language, as a social infra-language.[21] In the same way the 'Verdurin clique' provides a remarkable example of a codified language. Neither the 'stream of consciousness' nor the small focus of Paris life described by Proust can be fully understood if we confine ourselves to studying their significance in strictly literary terms. Useful, even indispensable, as methodology, the concept of code (or, more simply, language) would still not lead one to look on the novel as a kind of map with which a countryside may be reconnoitred but not actually known. Even if Albertine's sleep, or the Verdurin clique, are elements in a language of discourse, the psychologist and the sociologist are still obliged to analyse them rather more deeply than if they were objects rendered into language, representing, like the madeleine cake, model social-psychological functions.* Critical analysis which exploits only the one level of significant meaning does not seem to take enough account of the synthetic and analytic processes which arise from the novelist's own observation, processes which are part of his social sensitivity.

One final observation: the formalists, in concentrating on the text, have preferred for the most part to concern themselves with literature which is restricted in form – short stories, novellas and tales. Such studies emphasize the narrative facts rather than the large-scale complex structures of the novel.

*This idea is derived from Meyerson, *Les Fonctions psychologiques et les œuvres*, J. Vrin, 1947.

The problem of the absence of class-consciousness

The writer, it is claimed, never seems to be aware of being a member of a social class or of being dependent on it; yet class-consciousness is implicit in the whole body of his work. It is class-consciousness, with its accompanying contradictions (which the writer perceives without always recognizing them), which enables him to see, or rather, to receive and take note of, social facts of which he himself is not really conscious; it behaves rather like an operative concept. But actual awareness of the realities of the class struggle and of the conflict relationships of industrialism elude him. So his work distorts the true meaning of these social realities by transforming them into abstract terms.

Knowing how much the modern novel bears the stamp of subjectivism, it is difficult to refute such charges. Yet their very truth and generality render them ineffective, perhaps dangerous, when they appear in criticism. Could it not be claimed that the whole of Western art falls into this category? All literature is the product of writers whose class-consciousness remains inarticulate. A few exceptions – Paul Nizan's stories, for example – confirm this general law, for one cannot be sure that even Dos Passos, Sartre or Aragon were not more idealistic than Mann or Joyce. If sociology is the science of social facts as they are – of the way in which institutional structures develop and are demolished (which the novel is admirably equipped to describe), there is a danger that the sociologist may lean towards the self-same alienated and alienating system of ideas that he attacks in the writer, concentrating on getting down to the historical reality which is missing in the writer's work and obtaining that insight into the mechanisms of history which is denied to the writer because of his involvement in the 'value-system' of his own period. From this standpoint, the novel can no longer be regarded as 'containing' facts, or social and psycho-social relationships: their existence can only be 'discovered' in the text. The consequence is that what reality these facts and relationships have is taken to be a representation which is actually *masked* by the novel. Certain modern studies which start out, legitimately enough, to 'decipher' writings end up by surrendering to a cryptological demon.

Of course a novelist (tied as he is to one social class) can only display social phenomena, taking the word in its literal sense, to his readers. What he sees are *appearances*, and these are dependent, even in the way in which they are perceived, on his ideology – or on the ideological contradictions which possess him. Joyce and Musil both perceived social reality in terms of, and because of, their cultural and political exile. Bernanos and Malraux were also exiled, one in the name of divine grace, and the other by his distress at seeing his idea of universal man degraded. The most significant thing about Broch's novel is its title, *Les Somnambules*. The characters, haunted by the dissolution of 'values' in a dying civilization, sleep-walk with their eyes open through a world torn by economic crisis and shaken by class struggle. Broch's novel, however, is a summation of reality at a moment of history. If one wants to understand this moment one must try not to disregard somnabulism as a smokescreen but rather to take it literally, and then go on to deal with the art the writer uses in expressing it. The sociology of the novel should enable the history of a society to be read not *in* its literature, but *through* its literature – through the formally constituted literary artefacts it produces.

Is exile, or somnambulism, or whatever the general rubric is, to be regarded as part and parcel of the absence of class-consciousness in the writer, with the actual problems which the writer has failed to recognize revealed somehow in spite of him, through the medium of the kind of problems set out and discussed in his story? Is it the fact that the writer creates his own particular form of presentation out of the form in which they already exist in a primordial sense; i.e., the formulation of contradictions as they exist in reality?

This is undoubtedly the case if the novelist is regarded as somebody who belongs to a particular social class and is endowed with a particular culture. But when one comes to look at actual books, we have to ask how it is that the absence of class-consciousness in a Balzac differs from that in, say, Eugene Sue, or the same lack in Henry James from that existing in his friend Paul Bourget, or Virginia Woolf's from her 'enemy', Galsworthy's. The question arises because the sociology of the novel, whatever its cardinal rules and methods, must acknowledge the existence of two different, if not contradictory, types of realism: that which Lukács called 'critical realism', which applies to Tolstoy, Dostoyevsky and Thomas

Mann, and another form of realism which pretends simply to record reality, or to package it according to some artificial, usually 'moral', prescription, or, yet again, to transcend reality with some idea of subliminating, or merely evading, it.

The first thing to say about critical realism is that it displays the social driving force which Lukács emphasized.[22] The fact is that Joyce, Thomas Mann, and, especially, Balzac are novelists from whom one expects everything: their whole work constructs an all-embracing picture of society, including aspects of life which that society would prefer to keep hidden. Moreover, their novels portray characters who undermine the established social order and the values which that order, and they themselves, profess. In the same way, when we consider the whole output of Jules Verne, we find him illustrating all the characteristic values of industrial capitalism in full spate: the cult of science, of machines, of progress; the necessity of imperialism and its blessings; overweening paternalism; even racism. Yet the majority of Verne's major characters stand out against this contemporary world, setting off on solitary adventures which lead them either to death or into isolation from society. Many of his heroes contradict through their behaviour the ideological principles underlying all the tales of fantastic voyages. Often, it seems, Verne destroys the things he loves.

There are two possible ways of interpreting this curious contradiction. Perhaps the novelist, through this fundamental contradiction, is really communicating some pronouncement on the alienation of man under industrial capitalism? If we pursue this first line of interpretation, we would see 'displacement conflicts' being generated by the absence of class consciousness and the blindness to class conflict in the novelist; unaware that their fate, for good or ill, is actually being determined according to economic laws, these heroes of Jules Verne set themselves up in opposition to their own class, or desert it – but can only do so by exploiting the financial, technical or scientific resources they have been able to acquire by virtue of belonging to that class. Every one of Jules Verne's novels, according to this interpretation, is permeated by class-*unconsciousness* – which, of course, has to be there for it to be possible for critical realism to perform its task of uncovering the basic conflicts and the 'false solutions' (Captain Nemo, for example, withdrawing from

'Society' and making his attacks only on 'England') and going on to reveal to the reader the ineluctable presence of industrial capitalism, now in its imperialist phase, which naturally neither Jules Verne nor his heroes wish to recognize for what it is.

The second possible line of interpretation is that Verne, in narrating the fate of a Nemo or a Hatteras is really representing one of the essential parameters of every social group's existence – the mythical dimension, to which Lukács attached such importance. On this latter assumption, one interpretation of the fate of Jules Verne's heroes (who, when they do not die, turn into Robinson Crusoe masters of some tiny independent kingdom) might be that the ruling class is afraid – afraid in some profoundly religious sense – of the termination of its power, while nursing also the secret belief that its power can be redeemed by sacrifice.

This second interpretation, which does not exclude the first, seems to be sociologically and historically more correct. *Robinson Crusoe*, like *The Possessed*, embodies the concept of individuality. The value of the novel as a social document seems to belong primarily to the fact that it is the art form which gives the fullest and most profound account of the status of the individual at any given time in history. To say that a novel is composed essentially of characters (a proposition which Joyce, Proust and Virginia Woolf rejected some time ago) means that the writer embodies in them the social relationships which he has most frequently seen and experienced himself. But this personification occurs at two levels. One is specifically sociological: it has to do with the interaction between individuals, which, long before his commentators, the novelist, at least in the case of the writers of *Ulysses*, *The Diary of a Country Priest* or *The Planetarium*, knew very well were the codified rendering of a set of 'material' interests, myths or conventions. The second level is a derivative of the first, but is concerned with how the novelist presents a conception of life which is all-embracing and totally critical through the medium of one or two characters: the character connects with others through speech, that manifestation of himself which is most revelatory and which is immediately understandable; it is in this way that the writer displays social life in what is both its most obvious and its most secret modalities. The same character (Leopold Bloom, the Prince in the *Golden Bowl*, Bernanos' country priest) discerns what is wanting in these verbal social relationships to make them human. What is missing is what we call – and we need not stumble over the word – freedom, the successive changes of meaning and of form which are shown in their true colours by the novel, just as it shows us the evolutionary path – from jealousy to absurdity, from desire to free will – which is followed by all our psychological traits, or by our ideals or images of the world.

Robbe-Grillet is so definitive an example of this that he can be considered as a test case. In his theoretical writings, Robbe-Grillet charges Sartre with cutting himself off from 'the visual' which is the surest means of apprehending reality, and hence the most appropriate means of making ourselves free. Yet it was this same concern with liberty which was alive in Sartre when Roquentin, in *La Nausée*, put his trust in the feel of things and not in the sight of them.[23]

This brings us to an essential point. The novel is no more the work of imagination than it is a reflection of reality: its essence, its necessary quality, lies in the expression of the connection between the real and the imaginary. With Balzac, Dostoyevsky and Joyce, these connections are necessary and consistent. Their novels are not visibly divided between collectivity and individual, reality and dream, human depravity and the ideal, the base and the noble. Lukács' most important contribution to the sociology of the novel was undoubtedly in showing how the major works of fiction contrasted false values and authentic values. But this contrast consists only in the fact that the false values are degraded forms – of great utility to 'society' – of authentic values. The great novelists were able to uncover and to establish a logical relationship between the actual life of a particular status group, which adheres to certain ideals in a hypocritical fashion, and the behaviour of the hero, marked out from the rest and unhappy, who takes those ideals seriously and wishes to live by them. In sociology, the 'romantic lie' and 'the truth of fiction', which belong to the dialectic which we have just presented, are themselves facts. The same relationship obtains between the world of the whalers and the White Whale hunted by Captain Ahab as there is between puritan society and its thirst for the absolute, which it disguises as puritanism.

Novels which become dominant cultural creations are those in which can be read, between the lines of the surface account of particular human relationships, a general sociological theory covering a whole world of values which serves as a frame of reference for the hero's adventures and experiences but which is really much more than a frame of reference. Robinson Crusoe occupies himself on a desert island by reconstituting the civilization and the ideology of the Enlightenment, in which reliance on technology was linked with belief in Divine Providence. Again, Proust's Narrator is much more intent on understanding his own psychological make-up (an understanding which has some value for him) than on observing the aristocracy degrade itself for the benefit of the bourgeoisie which is out to acquire its attributes. Robinson Crusoe and the Narrator in *A la recherche* depict the overall status of the individual at one period of time and as a member of one particular social class. In the end they reveal a dialectical complementarity between social existence as it is and the myths which it generates, almost to the point of the myths being taken seriously and becoming values which give meaning to life.

If the lack of consciousness in the novelist reveals itself through this complementarity of the actual and the ideal, what can be said of lack of consciousness among those writers who assume for themselves what could be called a falsely critical realism – writing in Balzacian terms a hundred years after *Cousin Pons*, Stendhalian a hundred years after the *Charterhouse of Parma*, or Proustian a quarter of a century after *Remembrance of Things Past* ? One thing we must first be clear about is that the anachronistic content itself as well as the anachronistic form of these writings gives them a special kind of truth which makes the study of them of the greatest sociological interest. Indeed, the remark made by the anthropologist Boas is directly applicable to these novels: 'The thinking of what we call the cultivated classes is controlled by the ideals which have been handed down by previous generations'.[24]

We know that there are many grades of difference between realism which is radically critical and all-encompassing, and realism which is conformist. Cocteau and Giraudoux, for example, were non-conformist in regard to both middle-class tastes and its morals. Yet if we want to come to an understanding of bourgeois society in France – its languages and its values – at the turn of the century we have to turn to Proust. It is Proust we must read in order to understand exactly what contradictions prevailed in that world. In other words, the novelist we call 'great' discovers and establishes logical connections between the imaginary and what it rests on.

The artistic median

Realism which is totally, or radically, critical, however, always involves some innovative or revolutionary project within the art form. In the same way, the more vaguely realism is defined (the less it is concerned with the fundamental facts of society), the more clearly it reveals a traditionalist and academic conception of the art form. Céline, Faulkner, Benjamin Constant, all produced a sizeable number of successors who were themselves conformists. But from Flaubert to Beckett those novelists who were able to grasp the essentials of human relationships in a particular social milieu were also those who built up the novel into a work of art which had to be regarded as such from the very outset. With these writers, artistic requirements and sociological accuracy go hand in hand. A novelist is truly sociological when he is representing social phenomena which he has experienced at first-hand, and – this is the essential point – the 'code' of which he knows how to decipher. Those novelists who write within the bounds of the myth we recognize as culture are concerned exclusively with writing about what they know (the term 'myth' is used here in the sense employed by Lévi-Strauss: an organized collection of references to imaginary things which are yet logically bound up with real life). The course of social history itself explains the extensiveness of Tolstoy's range and the narrowness of Robbe-Grillet's. Yet both novelists were, in a sense, engaged in carrying out an actual social experiment, in that their books make explicit the separateness of the abstract notion of society and the existential actuality of social relationships. Through them, we are made to see what it is to live together under the cover of institutions and conventions – in brief, the forms assumed by society. It is the writer who illuminates the systemic aspect of 'living together', *Cousin Pons*, *The Ambassadors* and *Molloy* all establish, both implicitly and explicitly, that there is a distinction if not an incompatibility between the purely formal character of society (i.e. of a social order) and the ways in which the relationship between one person and another is lived out. The cast of fictional characters, and the hierarchic ordering, are worked out in terms of the ability (or inability) of each one of them to perceive this gap. Justine maintains her belief in the existence of justice in enlightened society in spite of the fact that a small secret society of monks, living under the protection of that self-same social order, abuse her body.[25] Awareness of the difference between society, in the form of its institutions, and actual social relationships brings about the downfall of the hero in *Wuthering Heights* – and the salvation of Vautrin, the only character in *La Comédie humaine* on whom Balzac bestows his own consciousness of the logical relationship between the structure of society in its entirety and the realities of social contact.

Yet the heroes of twentieth-century novelists, from Proust to Jean Cayrol, from Joyce to Saul Bellow are, for the most part, not concerned with escaping from the world (they are in fact its willing victims) but with withdrawing themselves from it: they choose to cultivate their own personal identity in secret rather than subscribe to social conventions and stereotypes. The last thing that Proust's Narrator wants is to be like Saint-Loup, who changes his character when he becomes integrated within a bourgeois status-group, and one of Jean Cayrol's characters would rather 'actually live other peoples' love' than go through the experience of a travesty of love, as they do. Throughout the modern novel, socially defined relationships and relationships between human beings are presented as incompatible. The 'deep structure' of the novel, from *Manhattan Transfer* to *Herzog*, lies in the opposition between society which is an abstraction made terrifyingly concrete in the programmed sequences of behaviour into which human existence is fitted and the manifestation of interpersonal relationships which are in some way or other wrested from the forms and constraints of the total society. This opposition constitutes one of the major themes of the theoretical writings by novelists on the art of the novel.

The choice of technical methods which will enable him to set down the experiences which brought him to realize exactly how 'society' differs from the 'social' is determined, in the first place, by aesthetic considerations. However little aware he may be of the socio-ideological systems that make up his image of the world, and which therefore constitute the primary model to which he works, and however ignorant he may be of the forms imposed on his creative mind by language, the novelist is nevertheless very much aware of the technical and artistic imperatives which control how he transcribes the way in which he sees himself and others. When Virginia Woolf remarked that the tools of Edwardian novelists (Bennett and Galsworthy) were no good for Georgian novelists (Joyce, Lawrence, and herself) she did not merely mean that new modes of expression must be found to correspond with a new social reality; a logical and consistent relationship had to obtain between observations and the artistic form into which they were rendered. Faulkner, again, speaks of his 'carpenter's tools' (among which he included violence) pointing out that the artist finds artistic means within social life itself. But Faulkner had read Joyce. Having listened to black children talking, he resorts to an interior monologue model to find a way of expressing the consciousness of the idiot Benjy in *The Sound and the Fury*;[26] we have here an institutionalized social form being converted into an artistic form by specifically literary means. Joyce, especially, devoted himself to the most wide-ranging study of literature before feeling able to take on the immense task of *Ulysses*. Yet again, certain works, like those of Balzac, Joyce and Kafka, serve as social and artistic models, if not moulds. By portraying in exemplary, paradigmatic, fashion their civilization at one particular stage, they become fundamental reference points for other novelists, like Döblin in *Alexanderplatz*, and Broch in *La Mort de Virgile*, both taken from Joyce's exemplar.

For the novelist, artistic and technical awareness mediates the way in which he understands social life – and its forms and codes. This remains true of even the least original novelist, who, we might say, makes unthinking use of his knowledge of the methods of Balzac or Céline in order to describe facts or to set down some autobiographical narrative. In both cases alike, the art and the technique of the novelist are social facts. The novelist writes for those who can read him, not for those who ought to. It is the form of composition, above all, which ensures that a particular work reaches the public for which it is destined, whether it is a work which is subversive, through its

exposure of actuality, or a conformist representation of society
(although there are also 'conforming rebels'). Of course, whatever
begins as subversion ends by being contained within bourgeois
culture, but, so far as the novel is concerned, what is subversive
seems to retain greater strength, even after it is integrated, than in
the case of the plastic arts: it is a fair bet that educated people are
better acquainted with Mondrian than with Joyce or Georges
Bataille. Genet's stories would be documentaries of sexual life in
prisons if Genet's writing (in which Chateaubriand's style is discernible) did not embody a violent poetry of eroticism, which of itself
constitutes a particular concept of any individual.

There is not, at any particular period, a great variety of images of
the world. It is easy to establish that one and the same fundamental
concept of the individual underlies novels as different as *Remembrance
of Things Past*, *Manhattan Transfer*, *The Magic Mountain*, and even
The Castle, insofar as the 'consciousness' of the individual in all
these stories stays, or endeavours to stay, outside the machinery
of society. Candide and Justine are brother and sister. Both believe
that all is for the best in the best of all possible worlds. In Sade,
tragic conflict lies in the writing; in Voltaire, irreverent conformity.

The different levels of the sociology of the novel

From what I have already written, it will be apparent that, for me, the
sociology of the novel has to be historical and comparative, the treatment of the novel as an artistic fact being of central importance. The
novel carries with it a truth and a reality which are notionally prior to
the novel: the conditions, including strictly economic conditions, under
which it is produced occupy an important place. Jules Verne's works
have four authors: the capitalist industrial society striving to swallow
up or to infiltrate the whole world; a scientific and paternalistic
ideology; a publisher who came across an author exactly right for
translating into a literary form this annexation of the world by the
West, this pushing of scientific discovery to its furthest limits; and
finally Jules Verne himself, who celebrates the takeover of the world,

SOCIOLOGIES OF THE NOVEL   73

yet works to subvert it through his often surrealist perception of nature and of objects and by his dedication to the myths of loneliness and of death.

The conditions of production for the novel are clearly visible in all this. It is impossible to disagree with Macherey when he emphasizes the fact that the conflicts within an ideology are transposed into literary works, and that consequently, by studying that self-same transposition, it is possible to discern just how this ideological conflict conditions literary production. Here, however, lies the difficulty: first, the conditions for its production have to be deciphered by reading the story itself; yet, secondly, the structure of composition of this story is not 'essential' to the explanation of these conditions, because the structure is only there to 'resolve in fictional terms' the ideological conflict transposed to the novel, so as to 'obviate its own collapse'. So we have to try to re-create, in summary form, the creative work of the writer in order to separate out the artistic structure of his novel from the material he has been working on.[27] We do not believe that the artistic structure of *Absalom, Absalom* is so absolutely inseparable from the novel as not to be able to reflect very clearly the ideological conflicts governing the production of Faulkner's novel – even when we take that structure to be no more than a carefully arranged disorder. However, Macherey's analysis brings two extremely important points to our attention. First, he demonstrates that it is impossible to confine structural analysis to the elucidation of the rhetoric (which is a way of organizing reality, not reality itself), and secondly that a sociology of the novel is something quite different from sociology *by means of* the novel; this raises the question of whether it might not be very useful to develop both kinds of sociology in a complementary fashion?

The novel contains within itself a reality and a truth which are, so to speak, meta-fictional – a reality and a truth quite distinct from, and over and above, the fictive world it presents. This is what seems to have been in E. M. Forster's mind when he stressed the dominating place which 'the life of values' occupies in the novel. Lukács made the same point. 'The life of values' is the same thing as a concept of the individual made explicit by the novelist. It is the meaning of his image of the world, the positive or negative significance he attributes to life; Stendhal's relativism, Proust's inner life are simultaneously modes of life and models for life.[28] But contained within that image of the individual are the bits and pieces which go to make up the reality and the truth proper to the fictive world itself: special relationships, social history, and the situation of the individual in a particular context. It is possible for the sociologist to study – particularly in innovative writings – how the population of fiction changes from one historical period to another: how, for example, the civilized and humane characters of the 1920s are replaced by the much humbler population called into being by Carson MacCullers, Céline, Graham Greene, Malraux, Bernanos and Lowry to portray the heights and depths of political and religious heroism. Only a few years separate Faulkner's vision of the American South tragically wrapped up in the past from the evocation by Carson MacCullers of the same region in terms of homely and humane pity, in stories no longer shadowed by the Southern aristocracy or by a jealous god.

Just as Panfosky followed the semantic evolution of the pastoral theme through the painting of the seventeenth century, so one might trace the changes of meaning and form of the notion of the absurd in fiction: clearly tragic in Kafka, the absurd becomes the rationale of living in Malraux and then Sartre; in Beckett the absurdity of life is 'like it is', while in *Le Repos du guerrier* it becomes convenient and rather comforting.

There is an interesting sociological study to be done on the character of the doctor in fiction. Revered by Balzac (because he knows the human anatomy as the writer knows the anatomy of society) the doctor thereafter is continuously de-mythified in the more stylistically original novels from Flaubert to Proust and from Céline to Reverzy. By contrast, there are any number of novels in the category of bogus critical realism which present the doctor as a noble soul whose conception of medicine as science battles with medicine as profit and with medical fashion. Today, 'hospital novels', selling in hundreds of thousands of copies, portray the inner conflicts which arise between the doctor's devotion to his patients and the doctor's emotional life. However, before a sociology 'of' the novel could become really meaningful, contents of the total production of works of fiction over a fairly long period would have to be analysed in a systematic way by means of appropriate techniques. (Although, again, one would be confronted with the obstacle of the unknowable; any publishing house can only publish a tiny proportion of the manuscripts it receives, whereas it may be that the sociologist should study all of them.)

There is, lastly, a further category of subject matter relevant to the sociology of the novel; the way it is read, and the various receptions and impacts it has within society. A sociological study of the reading public (which would only be possible in the context of a sociology of art) would make it possible to ascertain the different strata and different trends of the dream-worlds being manufactured within society, and to establish different kinds of socio-emotive models. Assuming that such a sociological study would be bound up with experimental aesthetics, and would be concerned with two main questions, 'who reads what?' and 'who expects to read what?', it should be possible to classify the displacement and protective phenomena taking place at the social level. To take one example of displacement: the heroes of certain novels are immortal, and some interest attaches to the way in which individuals, according to their social status, age or sex, recreate Julien Sorel or Raskolnikov for themselves in terms of their own view of contemporary social and political facts. In the case of projection, or identification: if we carried out a questionnaire survey of a particular population about what it likes reading, one could throw some light on the meaning and character of the readership reference groups mentioned earlier – meanings, and characters, incidentally, which are dependent on the system of production, for the majority of publishers prefer to publish their own particular 'type' of novel, and the notion of the 'series' has never been as powerful as it is today. In pursuing research of this kind, sociologists might come to see some justification for the argument advanced about the novel by surrealists, that it satisfies and stimulates the imagination of its public, but only by restricting it to the norms of 'plot', 'subject', and 'characters'. When someone is asked about his taste in reading, he reveals certain structural aspects of his imagination, or even of his whole mentality; it is not enough to conduct a market survey.

We end this account by making one reservation. There is no other art or type of literature that deals with as many facts of human existence as does the novel. However, we have to remember that when Forster enumerated the basic themes of fiction – which are also those of human existence – he mentioned birth, upbringing, love and death, but made no mention of work. This is a significant omission. Of course, the novel is more concerned with commenting on facts than on revealing them, but it remains true that Western fiction avoids work activity and work value. Work makes its appearance in novels in a rather artificial way, and man as worker dwells within them in some kind of implicit fashion. Work takes time, and time is needed for human relationships, and human emotions. There are few novelists like Hamp who would describe occupation, or like Roger Vailland, who dissects the apparatus of alienation from work in *325,000 francs*. Advocates of working-class literature were right in deploring the fact that Zola was overwhelmingly concerned in showing the wretchedness of work without showing it to be, at the same time, the source of socio-political consciousness.

If we accept Forster's pronouncement that the principal theme of the novel is nothing other than 'the life of values', we can proceed, appropriately, to the study of connection between the novel and myth.

CHAPTER 3

Myth and Fiction

THE myths of a people constitute an organic whole, a classified collection with formal structures which leave out of account, or contravene, aspects of time which we allow for today: regular intervals and divisions, progress and sequence, duration and development, history and change. There are no strict demarcation lines in myth between present, past and future. In particular, as the work of Dumézil, Lévi-Strauss and Vernant has shown, it appears that myth sets out the different states of being of a people, distributing them regardless of any development from one state to another. A popular myth creates the cosmos in which what we call human, or natural, or supernatural, are engaged in a vast but minutely particularized game of exchange and metamorphosis. Mythical thought does not present gods and men in opposition to each other. It deifies the human and humanizes the divine. A divinity is man's double on a higher plane, and, in symmetrical fashion, the animal and vegetable worlds are the doubles of the human world on a lower plane. However, the superiority and inferiority involved is not a matter of value but of level, or domain. The spatial world of myth embraces several distinct but interdependent zones, and it is in fact the task of the mythical tale to put this interdependence – of which the outcome is constant, cyclical and symmetrical – into words, either spoken or written.

There is one aspect of myth which is extremely relevant to the sociological interpretation of fiction: myth invokes the presumption of consistency to such extent that, theoretically, an infinite number of elements can be brought together and integrated in it without seem-

ing to be unnatural and without altering its individual structure.
Myth is open and closed at one and the same time. Oedipus remains
Oedipus, in spite of all the various guises and versions.

These qualities of consistency and elasticity in myth will receive
a good deal of emphasis, because implicit in them is the notion of
the episode, which is destined later to play so definitive a role in
fiction.

The divorce of the novel from myth

The ahistorical character of myth stands by way of corollary to the
notion of episode. In Hesiod, for example, we do not find the Ages
of Gold, Silver, Bronze and Iron treated as following upon one
another. The myth of the races of mankind divides human existence
among types of men and of functions, and devises a permanent
hierarchic order for the universe. The cycle has the Age of Gold at
its beginning, but is not started by it, and the Age of Iron at its end,
although this is not a terminus; indeed, the cycle is reversible. The
transition from gold to iron does not indicate decline nor progress;
each age is subjected to two forces which wage an eternal battle over
human existence: the order of justice, and the disorder of excess,
the former corresponding to fruitful peace, the latter to war and
destruction. These two forces, one pulling mankind towards salvation, the other towards destruction, operate everlastingly beneath
the eye of an omnipotent god, first Chronos, then Zeus. So it is that
men living at the time when the poet was writing could, if they had
had a King made in the image of God (i.e. just) realize that they were
living again a replica of the Golden Age as signified, for example, by
abundant harvests. If, on the other hand, the king and his subjects
were giving themselves up to excesses, men would know that they
were condemned to the Age of Iron – to an existence becoming more
and more wretched throughout a period of decadence and exhaustion.

It is the Age of Iron which marks the frontier between the ordered
and hierarchic domain of myth and the domain of temporal history,
in which, by contrast, it is impossible to make a fresh start, and in

which all things must move by degrees (upwards as well as downwards) towards death. The Age of Iron has to submit to time and to acknowledge it. It is the age in which man, left to his own devices in a world which is no longer of cosmic proportions, has to remember his successive deeds and achievements, and hence to invent, not history, perhaps, but at least chronicles and tales. In noteworthy studies, Meyerson[1] and Vernant[2] have noted that the transition from mythical extension to historical duration involves the specialized development of memory for psychological and social purposes. The kind of memory appropriate to myth does not require either the recollection or the preservation of past experience. It is total knowledge of what has been, what is, and what will be. It refers not to doing but to being, not to a series of successive happenings but to the mythical order itself – universal, structured, and classified. Each recital of a myth can only tell part of it; it is known that this one part refers to a totality. The American Indian myths collected by Lévi-Strauss appear to presume an analogous kind of memory – universal, repetitive, classificatory. The stories he records make up a total classificatory system where a complicated game of likenesses, complementarities and permutations takes place. Just as in Greek mythology, when what the Golden Age lost was gained by the Age of Bronze, or the statuesque quality of Hestia forms a symmetrical contrast with Hermes' mobility, so the Amazonian myths show us Orion and the Pleiades responsible for the appearance of fish, with Coma Berenices responsible for their disappearance. Again, if incest between brother and sister is the origin of the Sun and Moon, the alternation of the seasons is provoked by incest between mother and son. The moral of myth is that man can never have everything, for every transgression involves both loss and gain. The mythical order is made up of substitutions, compensations and correspondences.[3]

Nevertheless, myths are born and come to be developed in actual concrete societies – societies that are prey to wars, internal conflicts and, above all, to daily work and the remorselessness of time. Whether it be Greek or Amazonian, the mythical grasp of the world has two aspects – one of synthesis and totality, the other of analysis and fragmentation. Mythical thought implies the notion of everlasting recurrence. Myth conveys the everlasting duration of a theme together with the possibility of variations which, in principle, can be infinite. Hesiod's poem, the story of Asdiwal, or, again, the story cycle of Hercules, connect up the ideas of origins with those of structure.[4] But the diverse *content* of myth, the mythical tale narrated on its own, is a completely different matter. The vast structural order of a myth is composed of numerous narrative discourses filled with events. When one considers this analytical side of myth – this collection of adventures integrated within a single conceptual framework – it becomes clear that fiction existed before the novel.[5] Isolated, though not separated, from myth and epic, which may be envisaged as circular, the single episode foreshadows the fictional tale, which forms a line stretching from a beginning to an end. It is the need to include the episodic adventure in an ontological whole which is destined to ruin the inner order of the myth. When a fragment from a myth or epic is related, there is implicit reference to a larger order, but there is also disintegration of that larger order.

If we refer to the work of Dumézil and Vernant we find that they reject any incompatibility between history and structure, and refuse to isolate myth or epic literature, however ordered and self-sufficient they may be, from the actual institutions of society. One could make the broadest of generalizations, and regard the dependence-independence relationship of the part to the whole as foreshadowing and summing up the whole of our social history; fictional adventure being incorporated into the cosmos of myth, just as the monarchy is into mythology, the aristocracy into the monarchy and eventually the bourgeoisie into the aristocracy. Myth and epic correspond to social systems since, to achieve order and permanence, they need to establish symbolic and organic links between the ephemeral reality of human experience and the everlasting quality of the supernatural.

Fiction does not begin where myth ends. Human nature may be portrayed through fiction when it acquires a historically dominant status, or when men become capable of preferring the temporal and cumulative (though mortal) reality of their own actions to the everlastingness of the gods, of the supernatural – without, however, feeling the need to abolish this superior order, which may stay for a long time as their frame of reference. By means of history and the fictional story, mythical cosmogony may remain divided between the supernatural and the human, until the time when the latter eclipses the former. Yet this eclipse will be apparent only; the 'life of values' as Forster said, is just as necessary to the modern novel as the mythological order was to mythical tales when they were in the process of turning into fiction.

The hero becomes a character

The break-up of the mythical cosmos seems to have taken place in France during the middle of the twelfth century. *Brut*, the *Roman d'Alexandre*, *Eneas*, the *Roman de Thèbes* and the *Roman de Troie* are the 'five founding fathers of the modern novel', largely because their authors set out to produce historical works. Myth was 'historicalized' (the term used by Sartre eight centuries later to describe the essence of the novel) in this way because a new public had appeared. For political reasons this public was interested in history or, rather, was looking for a history; Henry II, for example, was concerned that history should show him to be the descendent of the Trojan Eneas, henceforth seen as the common ancestor of the Franks, the Normans and the Bretons. As the court became less and less familiar with Latin the history had to be written in French, which now became the language of everyday life.

The specificity of fiction is primarily a matter of language. Written in French, the romance translated myth and thereby brought its content closer to contemporary social life. Myths and legends were still composed and sung in the verse forms which allowed of the mnemonic devices so familiar, for example, in the *Iliad*. The romance, on the other hand, was intended for continuous reading, which, though perhaps not individual, was certainly private. The situation of the *geste*, the verse chronicle, and of the romance in the twelfth century, seems somewhat paradoxical. The epic tale, with its noble content, is addressed to a wide popular public. On the other hand, the romance, which often placed the hero in an everyday context, was addressed to scholars and nobles. This public, armed with new power, a new culture, and a new social status, which had to be confirmed and enforced, needed to acquire a literature which would both legitimate its position and articulate its conduct and sensibility.[6]

By endowing legendary heroes with the passions and chivalry of the knights of the twelfth century, by making these self-same heroic, mythical figures take part in the exploits of war or hunting appropriate to the Middle Ages, and by providing a setting for their heroes made up of castle keeps and tapestries, the transmutation of myth into romances introduced a psychological and social element which can still be found lingering in the work of La Fayette, of Sade and of Balzac – the element of identification. The reader is offered the opportunity of putting himself in the place of the hero. In the romance, which is historical in the most profound sense of the word, the idea of eternal recurrence becomes altogether eroded. The hero is taken at a specific point in his life, with time behind him and in front. From now on, therefore, he must be called a character, since he represents the individual person. To return to Meyerson and Vernant, this individual is a personality who no longer belongs to universal, undifferentiated, human kind or to a divine or semi-divine order. He is related to an established society with its own social order, its own system of social stratification, legitimated by specific values and ideals. The literary character represents a society and its different orders and strata, while the legendary hero was in no way representative. He was rather the substitute, the double, the deputy, of a magical or religious system. He had no history. He re-emerged constantly from (frequently to disappear again into) the eternity from which he had originally come.

Society and time are of the indispensable essence of the romance and of the novel. The novel provides a parallel between the divisions of past, present and future and the categories into which society is divided. But eventually these two kinds of dividing lines make the romance and the novel turn against those for whose benefit it was originally conceived. Although, in the first place, the medieval romance was intended to celebrate the social and cultural foundations of a particular class by defending and acclaiming the powerful, it constantly betrayed this primary function. For history does not only express the efforts of one particular group to establish itself in a position of power immediately below the ruler and above the common people. History is also concerned with what is to be; and the historical romance implies the possibility of social change. The *Roman de Troie*, for example, while explicitly intended to establish a social group half-way between the world of legendary heroism and its own recent history, contained the implication that those who had been defeated yesterday might become the victors of tomorrow. But, above all, the first readers of romances, who were also those who benefited from them, had to run a risk which might be called the risk of the imaginary dream-world. The authors of *Troie* or *Eneas* (unlike myths, romances had authors) humanized the notions of metamorphosis and of the 'marvellous'. They contrived somehow for their heroes, however supernatural they might be, to act out their parts in the real world. In committing such 'sins of anachronism'[7] these early writers of romances were following the same path as Tolstoy or Flaubert. They set universal values over against the world of observed reality. The dream world changes from the world of myth to a world of fantasy. The ideal world which one social group imagines today (or which it finds necessary in order to clothe its historical existence) may become the dream of another group, for which it will assume different forms and serve other needs.

In *Don Quixote* and *The Castle* one can follow the development of the relationship between a world of social reality, as represented by the characters, and a world of values. The compatibility or incompatibility between their two worlds is what distinguishes Balzac from Eugène Sue. As I see it, these are the two basic and conflicting standards which must be used in determining the value of the novel as a sociological document. In the *Satiricon*, for instance, we find a freed slave who has grown rich, fitting himself out with emblems taken from the legends, hiring his own poet and staging obsequies for himself appropriate to a demi-god. Yet all the people in the story, Trimalchion and his poet in particular, are only concerned with enjoying themselves and warding off death. Only Encolpe realizes that in such a world love must be dead, overcome by lust or self-interest.

One can find in Petronius' tale three essential components of the modern novel up to the time of the Second World War. In the first place a single class that has become dominant through the play of economic forces finds itself in a position to buy up and debase the appurtenances of a nobler past. Yet this plundering and debasement, of which Proust was so much aware, has a countervailing threat in the social mobility it engenders; for in order to show off its values and its new culture, and to enjoy itself to the fullest, the new ruling class has to do business with inferiors quite capable, in time, of destroying it. By the end, the saddened observer who has been given the opportunity of seeing all this has come to realize how much separates this perverted world from the authentic values by which he, and he alone, must seek to live.*

With the *Satiricon*, we find a new psychological and social function, a function which must be regarded as one of the main leavenings of later romance: the picaresque. The inferior (the serving man who is also observer) is well situated for stripping his master of the heroic finery and aura of piety which masks his lusts and fears. But before picaresque common sense despoiled the powerful of their borrowed prestige and suggested ways in which the commoner could take revenge on the aristocrat, fiction concentrated on trying to harmonize the actual way of life of a particular class with the ideals which it held. After adapting the supernatural world of myth and legend to the feudal world, the romance, as it became more and more historical, tended to humanize the feudal order by confronting the abstract code of courtly love with actual emotional experience.

So we find the moral principles of an immensely powerful and hierarchically ordered aristocracy exalted by Chrétien de Troyes to the level of a religious ethic. Yet we also find the heroes of *Erec et Enide* breaking the chivalric code; desire, in whose name all lovers are equal, triumphs over the code of courtly love. This liberating force of desire, with its recognition of psychological forces, was evidence of disturbance within the structure of feudalism itself. At the end of the twelfth century Robert de Buron, in adapting and distorting the spirit of Chrétien de Troyes, presents in *Lancelot* a

---

*One cannot refrain from noting that, in 1969 Fellini actually traced Petronius' route backwards. Originally meant to demystify readers and de-mythify society, the *Satiricon* was re-made for the screen in terms of mythical images. Yet these images are deliberately disjointed and incoherent; it is through them that Fellini expresses the essential character of a large part of Western society, a society which is fragmented and shattered yet held together by an economic system based on consumption of what is actually material, though assumed to be cultural or erotic.

hero who, confessing his adulterous love for Guinivere to an old hermit, is told that his sin began from the day that he was received into the order of chivalry.[8]

It was not, however, till the second half of the fifteenth century that a romance appears in which feudal ritual and the spirit of chivalry are unequivocally debased. In Antoine de la Sale's *Le Petit Jehan de Saintré*, a young knight treats the courtly code with perfect respect for the sake of his love. But one day his lady chooses as his rival a low-born abbé with whom the hero must fight with bare hands. Twice the abbé rubs him into the dust. This humiliating treatment of a knight who is made to fight with neither arms nor rules is not unlike the overthrow of heavily armed knights which had been achieved by agile infantry armed with bows and arrows.

But can one assume from this one tale, *Le Petit Jehan de Saintré*, written at the end of the Hundred Years War, depicting the spirit of feudalism assaulted and a vulgar bourgeois put on an equal footing with a nobleman, that a realistic essentially debunking type of fiction has been established which challenges class-based morality and proclaims justice and happiness for all? There is no place for oversimplifications of this kind; in the first place, the art of the novel, even with Zola, is always tied to a class system; secondly, the novel, from Cervantes to Robbe-Grillet, presents myth not as the opposite but as the counterpart of history. Balzac's writings are all related to the myths of contemporary society. Fabrice sees Waterloo in all its 'truth' and can show us the battle 'on a human scale' by virtue of the gulf he is bound to perceive between the epic figure of Napoleon and his own detailed, eye-witness view of the battle. But for this recognition of different levels there would be no 'realism' in that well-known episode from *The Charterhouse of Parma*. Stendhal's account of Waterloo is neither more nor less true than the scenes presented in *Les Misérables* which, at the other extreme, presents history as both myth and resurrection of the 'revolutionary' past of France.

We can think also of the bitter joy that seizes Roquentin in *Nausea* when he sees a single bare and twisted root, although he lacks words to describe it and imagination to embellish it. Thereafter, Roquentin becomes aware that reality is only existence and absurdity – two abstract notions which, however, become weapons for use against the

petit bourgeois torpor of 'Bouville'. Even at its most realistic, the
novel's purpose is never exclusively concerned with the destruction
of myths. The Russian people in search of a father, a father they
then seek to kill (for the father is by now no longer the Tzar) – is
described by Dostoyevsky well before the revolution actually accomplished the murder. Dos Passos writes about American society in
search of a past and in the basis of its being. Every novel must have
some myth to serve as a frame of reference and the question (which
Dos Passos, for example, and Sartre ask themselves) is precisely one
of knowing to what extent that particular myth is pertinent to the
actual historical society, and consequently can 'account for' it.

Through this necessary relationship between myth and the novel
an Hegelian conflict of master and slave is developed. In *Le Petit
Jehan* the order of chivalry which obliged the knight to face death for
what was now a futile cause is defeated by the bourgeois, who only
risk their lives for sound reasons and force the nobility to fight on
terrain they have chosen. But *Le Petit Jehan* also makes it clear that
the bourgeois-slave, on the threshold of a triumph which he still
enjoys, can only become the dominant knight by adopting values
comparable to those he is demolishing through work, technology
and trade. The writer of *Eneas* anticipates the longings of feudal
society by juxtaposing the world of heroes and giants and its actual
history. Yet through four centuries, up to the time of Balzac,
writers of romances and novels gratified bourgeois longings by
offsetting bourgeois energy and drive with values with names like
'liberty', 'individualism', 'deism', 'natural law', 'progress' or
'providence'. The picaresque novelists, who stripped the aristocracy and the powerful of their trappings and set them on a level
with the bourgeoisie, were only preparing the ground for the
bourgeoisie to build up a 'life of values' of which the aristocracy
were becoming less and less worthy. The day was to come when the
resurrected myth of Abélard offered to the virtuous, industrious,
bourgeoisie of 1760 the ideal goal for their emotions and, above all,
for their labours.

Myths reborn

Myths are destroyed; new myths are made. Jehan de Saintré is cast down only for the great solitary figure of Julien Sorel to be erected – to commit the error of not believing contemporary values are just a cover-up for the class system. The two conflicting, yet inter-dependent, tendencies in fiction are exemplified throughout *Don Quixote*. Marx rightly observed that Cervantes' hero 'expiates the sin of believing that knight errantry is compatible with any economic form of society'. Yet Freud is also right when he emphasizes the extent to which Don Quixote goes beyond the author's first intentions as soon as Cervantes provides him with the wisdom, the nobility and the determination appropriate to people who believe their ideals can be realized.[9] *Hamlet* and *Don Quixote* together make way for modern history by opening up gates through which the past can also sweep in. In *Hamlet*, it is the impossibility of tragedy that becomes tragic. in *Don Quixote*, the death of the epic becomes epic. Don Quixote (who is only familiar with epic through epic romances) tries to revive Amadis in full view of a petit bourgeoisie completely preoccupied with making things or acquiring things. He stands as a living reproach both to a nobility that has abandoned its values and to a petit bourgeoisie to whom he demonstrates that making history is not enough – there must also be ideals, emotions and a sense of the sub-lime. With his background of myth, which he believes is still alive, Don Quixote, accompanied by his 'real' double Sancho (who embodies the temporal world 'as it is'), sets out along paths which belong to history and which cannot survive long. In the end, myths will have to be constructed, a fact which the serene death of the poor knight himself makes clear enough. M. Robert has set out a clear case for making Kafka's works the logical complement – at the opposite end of the development of the civilization of modern Europe – of Cervantes' novel.[10] *The Castle*, especially, is a book in which myth is not a mirage so much as empty. If one compares the traps into which the heroes of these two novels fall, separated as they are by three centuries, as they press on to the limits of belief and logic one finds oneself dealing with two different accepted meanings of the word 'myth'. The models and memories of epic that

Don Quixote wants to revive still belong to the actual language of legend, with its own typology, its own ethics, and to a large extent, its own history. Amadis de Gaule does reflect, albeit pallidly, the language of Homer. On the other hand, the castle whose walls Kafka's surveyor tries to penetrate is a place that should express some rational unity between man and the world. Yet this place does not exist, or rather if it exists it is the very image of the absurd disorder that surrounds the surveyor in the village. The castle symbolizes the irremediable non-existence of a human setting that fiction had tried to reconstruct. Romance was created to establish living ties between myth and history. The function of the novel, thereafter, was the maintenance of connections between history and ideals (which must in this sense be termed myths). In *Wuthering Heights, Pamela, Marianne, Wilhelm Meister* and *Le Rouge et le noir* bourgeois civilization is able to read both its history, as it was experienced and fashioned, and the transformation of developing history into absolutes. Those absolutes, however, are both present and absent: luminous, manifest, and necessary, they are nevertheless marked out for death. Balzac makes Rubempré die an ignoble death. Prévost would have made him a model of sensibility; his death would have been presented as an edifying example. Madame de la Fayette's Madame de Clèves and Monsieur de Nemours would, fifty years later, have been crushed by the blows of a society that oppressed all manifestations of love and desire. From Marivaux to Rousseau, Goethe and even as far as Tolstoy (although in Russia only) one finds values which can be sensed, and which offer hope, but those who desire to attain them, or possess them, are consigned to death or resign themselves to loss.

It seems as if history would come to an end if ideals sanctified the human struggle directly instead of being realizable in some distant future. As I have remarked, novelists are the representatives and the betrayers of the bourgeoisie; they show that the perpetuation and the consummation of its labours and its business would be endangered if its ideals could be realized in the present, instead of being attainable only in the remote future. Heathcliff, Robinson Crusoe and Prince Andrei are all means by which society learns that it is futile to try to realize its ideals in this world, but that nevertheless humanity is lost if there are no individuals to undertake the endeavour. Western

European drama does not express the catharsis of the repressed so much as reproduce the sort of boldness fitting a society in which there is a desire for action on the grand scale, as with Lorenzaccio – without actually wanting to get killed.[11] It is in the eighteenth- and nineteenth-century novels that we find true catharsis; one must have ideals (not, be it noted, principles) but only on condition that they do not distract a particular social class from its historic and economic tasks. Saint-Preux and Julien Sorel are both committed to the affirmation of certain values and fated to perish (or be destroyed) on account of them. So society wins all along the line, piously pitying these heroes while continuing to live like M. de Volmar, old Sorel and de Renal.

It is this defeat that was perhaps in Lukács' mind when he made his observations on the social and sociological meaning of the novel. Lukács raised the question of how it was that the fictional character was obliged to discover the kind of order that belongs to myth, and why he had to pay for this quest with his life, his liberty or his soul. The same question which was raised by Lukács in terms of Marxist philosophy has been revived recently by Lévi-Strauss in terms of structural anthropology.[12]

The quest for Totality: Lukács and Lévi-Strauss

The idea of totality dominated Lukács work, from *The Theory of the Novel*, written before 1914, to *The Meaning of Contemporary Realism*. Following Hegel, Lukács saw the origin of this idea in Greece, where it was represented in art and literature by a harmonious image of humanity. Lukács found in Greek aesthetics, from which Greek ethics were derived, a close correspondence between form and content. Through their formal unity, literature and the plastic arts express a remarkable concordance between human life and values. Modern man, by recalling this total order of Greek culture – the wise and peaceful childhood of humanity – is filled with the desire to retrieve it. However, this longing has to seek fulfilment in a world no longer spatially restricted or institutionally united, like ancient Greece. The modern world, by contrast, is immensely complex, fragmented and disrupted by myriad contradictions. It is to this

world that the age of the novel belongs. The novel is essentially
concerned with describing the career of an individual in search of
some totality, some coherence, some identity, whose image he carries
deep within himself. This venture of his is doomed to failure since
there is no common standard, no mediation possible, between the
mentality of the hero and a world which is ruled by market values.
This contradiction, which it is the modern novel's task to resolve,
turns the fictional character into a problematic being. Unlike the
epic hero, whose exploits exemplify and embellish the accepted
values of his world, the fictional character sees himself confronted
with the impossible, while the possible still remains part of his being.
In thus stressing the ordered, categorical, stability of the ancient
epic texts, Lukács is in agreement with more recent students of myth.
Achilles and Aeneas were permitted to fulfil their true destinies, and,
throughout their travels, remained true to themselves. Characters in
novels, on the other hand, are always subject to alteration, even
though they remain in the same place; they strive incessantly to
reconcile a system of values with life as it is lived, although historical
(essentially economic) reality has for so long rendered them irremedi-
ably apart. The harmony which the hero of the novel seeks lies
irretrievably in the past. He sets out along a road, but the journey
is already over, says Lukács, showing in this how he has grasped the
profound ambiguity of the novel. From Tolstoy to Nathalie Sarraute
the search for values, or simply for truth, is always incompatible
with existing realities.

Lukács, however, has an historian's mind. He follows the changes
of the Western world as it moves further and further away from its
epic or mythical past. The ideals of a chivalric code which is dead
and gone conceal from the last of the knights errant the breadth,
diversity and complexity of sixteenth-century Spain; his fascination
with anachronisms renders his perception too restricted for the
realities of social and economic life. The great characters of the
nineteenth-century novel, however, are problematic for the opposite
reason – their perceptions are too wide for the actual world in which
they seek to work out their destinies. Lukács' comparison of Don
Quixote's 'narrowness' with other heroes who are 'over-extended' –
Julien Sorel, Jean Valjean, Anna Karenina, Prince Andrei or
Raskolnikov – is a superb sociological essay. Don Quixote, haunted

by a simple and straightforward legendary model, is, at the same time, the victim of a newly born bourgeois culture, characterized by innumerable conflicts and presenting a variety of aspects and activities with which his mind cannot cope. In the nineteenth-century novel the hero is in the opposite situation. At the beginning, he seems to have lost all memory of the happy unity of myth; he trusts society either to fulfil his ambitions or simply to enable him to live; but little by little, society (the society of a fully developed market economy) seems to him to be alarmingly unstable, fragmentary and disjointed in comparison with the breadth and unity of his own mind. Stendhal's, Tolstoy's and Dostoyevsky's heroes are confronted with a world that seems at times kaleidoscopic, at times mechanistic and at all times lacking any 'value' that could render it coherent. They end up by preferring the depths and complexity of their ego or super-ego to the fragmented soullessness of reality. Lukács' achievement consists in demonstrating how the characters of every one of the great novelists are people who come to learn what the difference is between the world of ideals and the world of historical realities.

Lévi-Strauss's views on the relationship between myth and the novel have a number of remarkable similarities with Lukács'. In the second part of the third volume of *Mythologiques*, Lévi-Strauss contrasts the coherent totality of myth with the linear narrative of fiction. The novel is characteristic of a civilization that lacks the order, the spaciousness and the logic of myth and yet seeks to re-discover them in an illusory historical progression. For Lévi-Strauss, as for Lukács, the world of fiction arises from the contradiction between enduring totality and changing history.

Lévi-Strauss' discussion of the transition from myth to the novel occurs when he is comparing two groups of American Indian myths which involve two kinds of periodicity – one made up of long annual or seasonal cycles, the other of short monthly or daily cycles. The first periodic form is characterized by diversity, the second by monotony. But myths related to the long cycles (for example, the origins of the constellations) and those related to short cycles (for example, the origin of the sun and the moon) are not independent of each other; the latter type of myth can be observed to be derived fairly uniformly from a transformation of the former, a trans-formation which 'affects more than the nature of the message'.

The construction of the story is also altered. The myths with short periodicity display a freedom of invention noticeably greater than their 'originating' myths. Observing that monotony stimulates the imagination more strongly than variety, Lévi-Strauss offers some speculations on whether this formal modification should not be seen as a transition or shift from the mode of myth to that of fiction. Indeed, the short myths offer 'a day-to-day' image of life (one that is constantly renewed) and remove man from the mythic system of multiple, though constant, relationships. Succession through time is substituted for regular and cyclic structure, and the hero of a myth 'decomposed' in this way can henceforth only survive in terms of a series of adventures.

These 'inferior' forms of myth are remarkably like novels, published in 'serial' form, a literary genre which 'a society which has committed itself to history believes it may be able to substitute for the magical natural order which it has deserted – or rather, by which it has been deserted'. Thus, serial stories present an upside-down version of the inferior myths. In fact, they disintegrate the coherent totality of myth. The 'inferior' myths do not have a real ending (for Lévi-Strauss, presumably, this represents a lesser evil); but the serial story tries, by rewarding the good and punishing the evil, to find 'a vague and caricatured equivalent of the closed structure of myth'.

We shall not attempt to discuss the question of whether or not Lévi-Strauss is right to assimilate the order of myth into the concept of structure; we only draw attention to the clarity with which he argues that the serial story derives from a nostalgic imitation of myth (to which, however, the serial gratuitously adds a completely artificial ending which is in accordance with its own ideals.) Even in its disintegrated form, myth still referred to a genetic and pri- mordial order. But the serial story gives an artificial order to human existence; and the not inconsiderable art of the writer consists in prolonging this process for as long as possible. The reader is carried along by a series of episodes which appear at fixed dates punctuating the regular cycle of his social life, torn between wanting and not wanting the series of adventures to finish; in any case, he only wants it to end the way he wants. Readers of Eugène Sue often wrote to him suggesting 'endings' and when the author of the comic strip *Juliette de mon cœur* let it be known – perhaps for tactical purposes – that he was going to get Juliette married off, his public begged him not to. If there is one genre that corresponds to Lévi-Strauss' analysis of episodic literature, it is surely the 'comic', based on the idea of the unending reappearance of the same character who yet, at every new appearance, has something different about him. Detective stories, again, with their investigations that resemble each other but are never quite the same, carried out by a detective who is always true to form, are proof that what excites the imagination is monotony – as Lévi-Strauss asserts.

Our own society seems to require myth in a form which is serialized, repetitive – and also Manichean, for at the end of the story, or of each of its episodes, an artificial good must triumph over an equally artificial evil. But society no longer asks for the expression of an ordered world or even a universal harmony from its myths. Modern society has indeed committed itself to history, and this prevents it from finding, except perhaps in dreams, an order that has been lost forever. At this point, Lévi-Strauss' approach fits in with the hypothesis advanced by Lukács. Quite logically, Lévi-Strauss sees the same relationships holding good between the serial and the novel as between the mythical stories which deal in short periods and the (structural) myths from which they derive. Because the novel is a historical narrative committed to the search for history's opposite, and so relates the adventures of a character who seeks a harmonious order which in fact lies in the past, it is bound, in most cases, to 'end badly'. We discover Lukács' problematic man once again: in the novel is expressed man's fatal inability to attain complete realization of his humanity.

Nevertheless, Lévi-Strauss' interpretation is not reconcilable with Lukács' theories. What keeps them apart is two conflicting conceptions of history. The anthropologist's approach is concerned with two notions which constitute the essential characteristics of the modern world and which figure among the major themes of the novel – progress, and industrialization. These Lévi-Strauss regards as malignant illusions. For a long period, the novel did have a messianic role; it reflected faith in progress which would enable ideals to be realized, ideals which would themselves replace the order of the mythical world. Thereafter, the novel was applied to the denunciation of the unanticipated results of 'history' – the crushing and enslavement of humanity by industrialism. Lévi-Strauss also makes rather fleeting reference to a phenomenon with which all the great novelists of the first thirty years of this century were much concerned – the parcelling out of individual identity by a mechanized and utilitarian culture. When he remarks (no doubt thinking of the 'new novel') that after having watched the domination and debasement of the novel by its plot, we are now watching the downfall of the plot itself, he is only raising once more the problem of the coherence and finality of human destiny, which forms the subject of most controversies concerning modern fiction, certainly from the time of Proust and Joyce. At least Lévi-Strauss can take some credit for raising the problem within the framework of anthropology. He is concerned with the same question which, from a totally different perspective, had concerned the characters in the *Noyers de l'Altenburg* – the question of the unity of humanity. Western civilization, completely preoccupied with its own history, despising other civilizations (seen as objects of study) is heading for final non-entity – and its novelists testify to the fact.

Structure is not to be discovered through history

Yet it is difficult not to see the value judgements contained within Lévi-Strauss' analysis. His view of the Western novel, especially the contemporary novel, is not without its normative aspect. He seems to present the novelist (the interpreter of civilization) as a kind of renegade who, in fact, repudiates myths, although he is trying to rediscover the essence and the form of myth. In the third part of *Mythologiques* we are reminded of the tone of Rousseau's *Lettre à d'Alembert*; like the theatre for Rousseau, the novel for Lévi-Strauss seems to carry a sense of evil, an evil which lies in the abandonment of the state of nature – by which is meant harmony between man and man and between man and his physical environment.

Lukács, on the other hand, believes that the mythical order (of Classical Greece, that is) persists as a frame of reference which is not to be rediscovered except through history. When history 'comes to an end' the human harmony mirrored in Greek civilization will be realized. History is not a process of degeneration from a coherent cosmogony, but a necessary development which man is bound to further. The sense of history, regarded by Lévi-Strauss as perverse and vain, is for Lukács a sign of human power. If the novel expresses an unrealizable desire for universality it also expresses the fact that universals really exist, however disguised. The very fact that the fictional character reveals the contradiction between reality and values, and tries to resolve it, thereby merges him with the consciousness of his creator. By virtue of his *Weltanschauung*, the novelist approximates to what Lukács calls 'potential consciousness', the consciousness we would have if we could grasp the economic and social facts of our present historical situation in all their complexity.[13] By showing that a whole series of veils exists between history as it is, and history as it ought to be, the novel shows that history is not in itself evil – history is the gradual realization of the fullness of man.

Evidence for this is found in the evolution of the novel. Debased epic to begin with, it soon regains the coherence which belonged to myth. Lukács had already provided the response to Lévi-Strauss when he showed that the Western novel, up to the end of the nineteenth century, and even up to *The Magic Mountain*, had not always sought the revelation of pristine universality in vain. In one 'problematic' period Tolstoy and Dostoyevsky created new forms of epic.[14] These forms were not imposed arbitrarily on contemporary life, and they do imply the possibility of human fulfilment.

Novelists, from Cervantes to Thomas Mann, were able to criticize their own times, in so far as they were capable of comprehending them at all – by showing man in all his aspects. Critical realism is the ability to bring to light all the contradictions, conflicts and ambiguities of humanity at a particular moment in time. Lukács, with extraordinary insight, makes a distinction between the generic typicality characteristic of naturalism and the 'profound typicality' found in *Anna Karenina*.[15] Similarly, the value of *Dr Faustus* lies in Thomas Mann's distinction between the lighter and the darker sides of a person and his nature under the aspect of history and of myth.

When Lukács used the title, 'Thomas Mann or Kafka?' for one of his chapters in *The Present Meaning of Critical Realism*, he was asking a question of considerable sociological and political significance. Later we shall emphasize the fact that Kafka sapped the foundations of the whole of Western fiction from Cervantes to Faulkner, for the courses followed by his stories and their endings show us that man can no longer conceive of values which might protect him from the 'nightmare' of history and eventually free him to achieve full humanity. Through the rigorously linear sequence of events in his stories, which makes manifest the futile confrontation of the irrationality of the universe by individual reason, Kafka obliterates Prince Andrei's dream, as well as the splendid isolation of interior monologue. He makes the realization of the total potentiality of man inconceivable. Yet one wonders whether this reduction to absurdity is sociologically and politically valid. Remembering that Thomas Mann and Kafka were contemporaries, which of them had the right view of reality – the novelist for whom humanity was varied, complex, contradictory, and therefore vital and susceptible to change, or the other (as middle-class as Mann) who was already anticipating Marcuse's one-dimensional man?

This reference to Marcuse enables us to make some observations on the dilemma posed by Lukács: is the modern world so uniform and passive as to extinguish the spirit of critical realism in writers, or are the writers themselves, as in the case of Kafka, so fascinated by man that they forget that the world is still varied and turbulent, still the arena of the class struggle, and, consequently, that man can still be represented by the writer in terms of universality and multiplicity? For Lukács, Kafka's man is a myth, artificially isolated from human kind, which carries on its hidden life, with all its contradictions, conflicts and hopes. Lukács also charged Beckett (as he would doubtless have accused Robbe-Grillet) with idling away the time instead of confronting reality. Unlike Thomas Mann, Beckett (and perhaps most of the important Western novelists and dramatists of the 1950s) preferred to settle into 'the luxury hotel of the Absurd' rather than show any interest in the real world.[16]

Lukács is clearly more at home with Thomas Mann than with the 'literature of the Absurd', which seems to alarm and disturb him. His examination of this literature is certainly less objective and less far-reaching than his studies of European realism in general. The fact is that Lukács' special concern (although it hardly amounted to messianic dedication) is with the novel's expression of the meaning – the march – of history, and of society in change. Thomas Mann's stories contain and present 'perspectives'; it is these which are obliterated by stories in which the idea of the absurd is both theme and ultimate viewpoint. While Lévi-Strauss regards the novel as expressing the powerlessness of the Western world to realize the unity and harmony of humanity, Lukács believes that Western writers are betraying their proper universalizing mission, the mission defined in *Don Quixote*, *Anna Karenina* and *Faustus*. Both, in the last resort, interpret the way in which 'characters' have been eliminated from the novel as a sign of the debasement of the idea of personal identity in a society in which it has become merely a word. Lukács understands that in becoming a literary theme, the idea of the absurd refers not so much to an existence stripped of meaning as to human relationships deprived of consistency and the ability to communicate.

Finally, we may note, Lucien Goldmann's very different interpretation of the 'absurdity' of the novels of the 1950s (made, in fact, with reference to Lukács' ideas, and in particular to the idea of reification). According to Goldmann, Robbe-Grillet, for example, far from making absurdity into something special, or an alibi, is expressing the essential quality of reified and passive social relationships. The difference between these interpretations seems to lie in the fact that while Lukács regards myth as at one with human nature, so that mythical thought carries within itself revolutionary thought – or at least the need for social revolution – Goldmann, on the contrary, considers myths as engendered by different class situations as they succeed each other in history.

The modern bourgeois epic

Study of the sociological significance of the novel has to start from the dichotomy which occurred in mythical thought and literature. The conceptual division of myth produced two modes of fiction –

one corresponding to the disparate episodic contents of the great myths or epics, the other retaining their overall sense as a frame of reference, a sense which is cosmic and ontological. The first mode produced an immensely varied and numerous class of fiction concerned with the organization of events, rich vicissitudes and reversals, meant to make the reader believe what is ultimately illusory even (Robbe-Grillet says especially) when illusion takes the form of 'realism'.[17] The second mode includes those writings that reveal the perpetual quest through history for a being or essence completely independent of our historical selves. Lukács, however, has shown how the object and meaning of this quest have changed during the period from *Don Quixote* to *Anna Karenina*. The idea of the 'consciousness' of the possible could equally well refer to a particular writer's view of the essential relationship between certain historical social conditions and one ideal or set of values which happen to be caught sight of and pursued. The society in which Tolstoy's characters live presents possible ideals while preventing the same people from realizing them. The same thing applies to Proust's Narrator, Broch's 'sleepwalkers' and to Leopold Bloom.

Critical realism cut a path for itself through illusory realism at the time when the bourgeoisie was invading and undermining the monarchical order. In the seventeenth and eighteenth centuries, the conventions – in the pejorative or 'mythical' sense of the term – of fiction were established by those stories whose structure was a generalized reproduction of the structure of the Map of Love.* There was nothing vague or romantic about this kind of story. It was the product of calculation. The author lays a series of traps for his hero which serve as barriers to his rightful pursuit of happiness but which also serve to bring out his moral and emotional worth in the face of ordeals. Such a hero – whose perfection aroused the sarcastic comment of the Abbé d'Aubignac as early as 1660[18] – wins the right of happiness just as Ulysses wins his right to return home; from a labyrinth of ordeals he suddenly finds himself free to enter 'normal' – i.e. aristocratic – life.

*Mademoiselle de Scudéry and her circle in the seventeenth century invented a game called *Pays du tendre*, to whose territory the *Carte du tendre* refers in her novel *Clélie*. The phrase was seized upon by her critics as a sign of preciosity and is a familiar reference in French literary history.

During the period of the enlightenment the novel of intrigue was gradually displaced by the novel of manners, whose final success came in 1760 with the publication of *La Nouvelle Héloïse*. As Moinet has shown[19] Rousseau's novel brought to an end a lengthy debate on the usefulness of the novel. The novel of manners, which dealt essentially with contemporary life and was peopled with characters concerned with actual psychological and social problems, proved its worth by expressing in concrete terms three values on which the bourgeoisie founded its endeavours – work, sensitivity, progress.

Marivaux, Richardson, Fielding and Goethe produced stories that were fundamentally didactic. The novel of manners is primarily concerned with the realities of life, with its concerns, its setbacks, its work, its conflicts of persons, interests, and classes. No kind of person, no class of things is by definition excluded from such novels. As Rousseau wrote in the second preface to *La Nouvelle Héloïse* one should: 'depict all the varieties of human nature, even monstrous and extraordinary creatures', and 'what each of us can see every day in his own and in his neighbour's house'. The novel of manners also asserts everyone's right to happiness, since depth and nobility of feeling have nothing to do with birth. Especially, the reader comes to perceive history as history that, step by step, is advancing towards the unity of mankind, a unity which is to be realized in the triumph of value. Even before *Wilhelm Meister*, the novels of Fielding and Marivaux had didactic elements that were educational in that they were permeated with the idea that history has direction and meaning. The reader follows the life-story of a character because it moves in step with, and assists the progress of, history towards justice. And if this character is a 'man of sensibility' it is because only 'sensibility' can engender and guarantee virtue. 'Sensibility' is an integral part of a morality which consists of a sense of justice and a love of mankind as much as of work. Living should mean learning. The most trivial and minute (and often the most irksome) aspects of social life are but microcosms of a whole historical destiny.

Between about 1720 and 1760 the novel of manners, by virtue of its prophetic message, gradually overcame the novel of intrigue. 'There is nothing realistic about realism', remarked Sade, commenting on the novel during his own century; he was the only novelist then to make a distinction between the myth of virtue and the myth of the inevitable progress of history towards a happy ending. Yet what would *Juliette* be without the myth of sexuality which so curiously anticipated the myth of social Darwinism?

The great success of *La Nouvelle Héloïse* was largely due to the way in which Rousseau dealt with the prophetic notion and its implications; even if sensibility, fraternity and humanity had not yet been completely accomplished evidence of their presence was certainly there. The bourgeoisie (and a few aristocrats who had understood the lessons of middle-class faith in work and the middle-class ethic), found itself reflected on a larger scale in a book in which the rational exploitation of the land, the manufacture of artefacts, and the liberalization of relationships between masters and workers were taken as being actually achieved. *La Nouvelle Héloïse* is fundamentally a product of the Encyclopedists' view of the world. Man is shown to have command by virtue of his wisdom, industry and generosity. Man as a social being and man as producer are one and the same. One critic, Mercie, remarked of novels in 1784 that they painted 'imaginary pictures of social happiness'. But to his picture, which offered readers a credible and applicable model of working conditions and human relationships (in contrast to Fourier's futuristic system) Rousseau added the portrayal of a social and psychological phenomenon destined to play an essential part in the novel – the phenomenon of sublimation, which means renunciation.

In the *Confessions* Rousseau observed: 'I identified myself with the lover and the friend as far as I possibly could.' Such identification was something generally expected of those whose love was thwarted because of social barriers and then went on to ask themselves why it was that sensibility and enlightenment were no longer compatible. Rousseau set up a positive model in contrast to the negative model of des Grieux in *Manon Lescaut* – the transformation of individual passion into love of humanity. When he revived the myth of Abelard in the book, Rousseau was as much a realist as he was in describing a working community on Volmar's estate. The force of passion and sensibility is as strong in *La Nouvelle Héloïse* as in *Marianne*, but in one case it is stifled because the class system renders it 'impossible', while in the other case it remains, developing and flourishing ideally, platonically. When this happens, love is manifestly not victimized by society which, indeed, remains 'good', by which is meant 'progressive'.

Rousseau, as novelist, can be regarded as making a statement about human and social relationships in a society which is trying rather ineptly to conceal its own materialism and instrumentalism. Two rather depressing lessons can be learned from *La Nouvelle Héloïse*: first, the belief that the heart can triumph over all social obstacles is a delusion; secondly, if 'sensibility' is to contribute to the realization of a truly humanist society, passion will – frequently at least – have to become transformed into 'virtue'. Made part of the myth of 'The Good', the renunciation and sublimation of love provided society with a convenient value; sublimation offered a half-way house between the promises of the philosophers of the Enlightenment and a reality which could already be rendered in terms of social and economic forces. The virtue of emotional renunciation thus came to be added to, and to reinforce, the work ethic.

In a different social milieu, another myth was acquiring the same kind of relevance – the myth of evil, exalted and condemned by Laclos in another epistolary novel. Just as the bourgeoisie, having won recognition and legitimation for its code of virtues, needed the myth of good, so the lower ranks of the nobility needed the myth of evil – its *Carte du tendre* of the world of pleasure. Monsieur Volmar, however, can proceed with the rational exploitation of his lands. He is moving into the future, whereas there still exist, even today, laws and a social system to punish the erotic transgressions of a nobility that retains no more power than resides in the licentious vocabulary it uses.

The 'modern bourgeois epic' depicts the 'conflict between the poetry of the heart and the prose of social relations'. But this conflict, as Hegel says of the novel which he defined with these words in his *Philosophy of Art*, is not always resolved through tragedy. A hero can be reconciled (and this is Hegel's preferred solution) with society. Faithful to the Enlightenment, Goethe makes *Wilhelm Meister* move gradually towards the accomplishment of the union of the individual with society, neither of which has any value in isolation; they are dependent on each other for full realization. Rousseau, who was more of a realist, had shown in the person of Saint-Preux the social and emotional price that had to be paid for such a union. (In Forster's words, novels console us; they present us with mankind made intelligible.) With Rousseau, an aspect of reality enters literature which is destined to take on a growing importance in the novel – the fact of failure. The explanation and rationalization of failure is the central purpose of many modern novels.

The myth of Goodness, which Rousseau, who was looking to the future, made so much of; the myth of evil, consciously fabricated by the protagonists of *Les Liaisons dangereuses* (who in fact were living in the past) – what reality do they really have in connection with the development the objective facts, of the social order? None, is Balzac's answer, delivered after revolution and counter-revolution had wiped out both enlightened despotism and the social contract.

Balzac – the plateau

The only myth in which men can, or should, believe, is that of society; the only reality conceivable is that of social relationships – Balzac is the first and the last novelist to effect a precise reconciliation between myth as the timeless realm of truth, and fiction as the reality afforded by historical time. In terms which evoke, and invoke, society so that it becomes a 'hidden god' whose presence – invisible, inaccessible and indifferent – presides over the enactment of tragedy, as Lukács suggests, Balzac makes society man's whole life, his be-all and end-all. In *La Comédie humaine*, society seems to express the fundamental characteristics of the recorded myths which were the subject of Lévi-Strauss' studies. It constitutes an enclosed, graded, categorized system within which constant transformations, permutations and combinations occur.

Fascinated as they have obviously been by the scope and diversity of Balzac's world, most of his critics have failed to put sufficient stress on the relationship between stability and change on which it rests. Basing his work on the idea of society in its entirety, the novelist assumes that the social order has reached the last stage of its development, or at least a definitive form and structure. The 'human comedy' and its multiplicity of acts and scenes, which all represent different categories, is a kind of testament made at the close of history, signed and sealed jointly by religion along with monarchy. However, the social structure which has been stabilized in this way is constantly renewed, like cells in an organism, by individual destinies, which Balzac organizes into two distinct and incompatible species.

There are two categories of Balzacian hero; the first is of those who are blind to the fact that society is a machine of interlocking wheels driven by two motors – the principles of profit and the will to power. Characters in the second category serve this machine and adjust their lives to its motions. The former are lost, the latter saved. These two major groups of characters may be subdivided according to whether or not they are conscious of society as an all-encompassing truth and system of reality. All, nevertheless, are equally ambitious, Pons the collector as much as Rastıgnac the tactician, Vautrin the strategist, and Rubempré, desperate for glory. While one group's ambitions are founded in desire, the other's in calculation, in both cases the individual is entirely a reflection of what is happening in society, just as society reflects the individual.

It is society that sanctions the individual's conduct and passions, rewards Vautrin for making himself its servant and punishes Rubempré for loving Esther. Balzac reduces all the human hopes and illusions that have been incorporated into his myth of society to social terms. Yet not every character in Balzac can be called Balzacian. He usually confers the status of archetype on to strongly individualized characters, who, by virtue of their strength, express the specifically social qualities of human personality – its basic sociological condition. Each character that Balzac puts in a prominent position represents one element in the social organism, whether he is favoured by the forces of social determinism (because he is fully aware of them) or becomes their victim (because he is ignorant of them). Yet leaders of society, like the Popinots or the Granlieus, are so close to the throne and the altar they do not seem to be part of the system. Perhaps it is because they really control it.

Confident of his ability to reconstruct the whole of society from one element, as Cuvier reconstructed a prehistoric animal from one bone (an image used by Balzac), the novelist saw himself as not so much portraying a society as constructing an explanatory sociological model of the individual. He worked out his design in structural

terms and the sociologistic frame of reference he sets up was
enormously influential. Western European and American fiction and
the cultural world it contains became, after Balzac, dichotomized,
one defined in terms of the Balzacian *Weltanschauung*, one in terms
of its denial.

The influence of Balzac

The *Comédie humaine*, in fact, established a representational model
for fiction, a model which met the same fate as the model for painting
established according to the laws of perspective; after producing a
transformation in art which amounted to a revolution in thought and
manners, the idea of perspective eventually came to uphold an
academicism consonant with the established social order. The
'Balzac effect', reinforced by naturalism, is still powerful in a cultural
world which still includes Nuncingens, Gaudissarts, poor relations,
social groups, which all keep themselves going or go under, as they
did first in the *Comédie humaine*. Sinclair Lewis, Upton Sinclair,
Theodore Dreiser, Galsworthy and Bennett kept Balzac alive, as do
the majority of best-sellers. Yet, if our world contains many people
and social phenomena that call for Balzacian treatment – the presentation of a character in terms of his ambitions, his context, his
physical appearance and his psychological characteristics – this does
not mean that Balzac's structured and deterministic cast of mind is
still appropriate. Between Balzac's work and the narrative forms for
which it stands as a point of reference and a model, there is a gap
similar to the gap found by Lévi-Strauss between myth and its
debased forms. Over the last hundred years, innumerable novels have
been published which are modelled not on Balzac's vision of a
categorized graded society in its entirety, but only on the content or
the structure or the schema of the *Comédie humaine*. The canvasses
are filled with the picture of a family, in the perspective of space and
time; the subject-matter is like Balzac's, social and psychological,
but treated in quite a different way. In Balzac, society as a whole and
individual passions are two radically opposed aspects of human

nature, which can only co-exist if individual desires subject themselves to the determinism of social forces. In these derivative novels we find that society no longer exists as an organism ruled by economic laws and moving according to its own mechanism; society merely becomes social happenings. It becomes an undifferentiated mass assimilated to the human condition, no longer of law but of accident, or fate. The logical relationship between personal desires and the machinery of society observed by Balzac no longer exists. In these derivative novels we find, for example, personal feelings crushed by the power of the bourgeoisie or by 'money', or perhaps the strong generous individual resisting oppression by his 'milieu' or by his 'family'. Balzac's typification – and this is the essential point – is replaced by characters.

But although such works – of the kind which Proust, or Melville, could never have written – are sociologically false, they nevertheless reflect with reasonable accuracy the social and psychological models which obtain among bourgeois and petit bourgeois, models which are only gradually modified. The Balzac type of novel still bears some resemblance today to a world which sees society as a necessary condition – a necessary evil; all societies are bad, and set the strong against the weak, the mean against the noble, the defenders of order against the partisans of liberty, and money-grubbing against unselfishness. Balzac-type novels are documentary in the strict sense of the term; realism in them amounts to a criticism of forms rather than fundamentals, and the idea of social situation eclipses the idea of social class. They appeal to readers of the kind who like to see the brutalities of army life denounced (although 'as long as there are men, the army will be like that'), or the tragic consequences of marriage between a provincial bourgeois and a young girl from another milieu condemned. Society suffers diseases, so health is feasible. Social psychological disorder is the price that must be paid for the maintenance of social order compatible with the existing material order.

Virginia Woolf, therefore, was both right and wrong when she rejected as anachronistic Galsworthy's 'tools' and the aesthetic principles of Arnold Bennett, for whom 'all good fiction was based on the creation of characters and on that alone'.[20]

She had no desire to regard English bourgeois society in 1920 as comprehensible in naturalistic and Balzacian terms: the conflict or conjunction beteen the substructure of an industrial society and the emotional lives of individuals still existed to justify narratives in which existence, particularly the life of families dependent on social relationships and social events, was expressed through characters. On the other hand, Virginia Woolf was right in that the point of view, the system of constructing social reality, implicit in *The Forsyte Saga* avoided the actualities of human relations, and failed to explain their meaning.

In setting her face against Galsworthy and Bennett, Virginia Woolf was joining forces with a tradition which can be traced back from Joyce to Dostoyevsky, from Conrad to Meredith and from Melville to Jane Austen. The tradition is anti-Balzacian, it is related to Stendhal's *Weltanschauung*, which explicitly contradicts the determinism of the *Comédie humaine*. Rastignac knew how to live as society wished to. Julien Sorel contrasted the ideals which served as a front for society, in general, with the actual practices current in a particular milieu. Balzac invents society, Stendhal, interpersonal relationships. Balzac stage-manages society ('surely the world is a theatre?' he says in *Splendeurs et misères des courtisanes*), while Stendhal puts himself in place of the actor and the spectator and the impresario of the social drama. For Balzac, society is master of human passions in a systematic way; for Stendhal, society and the subjectivity of the individual are completely different and irreconcilable, and there is absolutely no reason why one should be of less worth than the other, or should give way to it. Yet Stendhal does seem to give more emphasis to the sociological (as distinct from 'the social') perspective, perhaps, than Balzac did. Indeed, the fate of Julien and Fabrice is determined from the very first by the idea of social advancement, which the figure of Napoleon, as the man who fulfilled the liberating, egalitarian revolution, stands for. But the idea of advancement in the social world is, for the Stendhalian hero, of universal application; accordingly it applies to his private life, and there comes a day when his strategy of social advancement is actually destroyed by the consequences of his strategy in pursuit of private passion. The result is that the hero comes to see 'Bonapartist ambition' as a false myth, and the myth of his own emotional ambitions as true. At least the latter stems from himself, while ambition in the ordinary sense seems absurd and pointless in a world in which 'reactionary' conventions had been re-established. The Restoration, for which Napoleon had paved the way, made it impossible for the Bonapartes of the world.

The collapse of a social myth encourages the promotion of a private myth. The process is discernible in both *Remembrance of Things Past* and *Ulysses*; it is further evidence of Lukács' penetration in contrasting the narrowness of the modern world with the complexity and breadth of sensitivity revealed by some observers. After Balzac, genuinely critical realism ceased to be 'Balzacian' because the dissonance between the actual world of interpersonal relationships and the level of a world in which ideals could be entertained became increasingly obvious. Seeing how social relationships cheapened consciousness and sensitivity, Tolstoy's and Dostoyevsky's (and, later, Joyce's) characters turn to questioning values on which such relationships are supposed to be based.

Truth in concealment

Starting with the contrast between Balzac and Stendhal, we find the novelist and the fictional character following divergent lines of development and adopting contrasting positions. Balzac may not have been the inventor of 'the type', but he certainly worked out a typology of society. The aim of his predecessors was to unite in a single fictional character the attributes of society and of the individual. He worked towards the same end, but with the gloss of cynicism added. Rigorously constrained within his sociological framework, his characters destroyed the didactic novel with its messianic message, although it was reborn in the twentieth century in *The Magic Mountain*, *La Mort de Virgile* and *Ulysses*, this time looking to the past rather than to the future. Yet the Balzacian type, even if 'objectively' cynical, never transgresses the laws of society – especially when the type is a Vautrin. The desire, the will of a Balzac character is much more to be integrated into society than to impose his personality on it, or to depart from the rules of conduct obtaining for the appropriate social class. The Balzacian will is will to position, not will to power; it is the complete opposite of the 'Napoleonic' will. The Stendhalian hero, by contrast, is involved with the concept popularized by Durkheim – *anomie*, a condition which often marks the tragic hero. The framework of laws, institutions and rules is too narrow for the Prince of Homburg, for Lorenzaccio or for the hero of *Tête d'or*. Julien Sorel also belongs to this group, but through fate, not by design. Sorel did not begin with any intention of transgressing the laws of society; he wished merely to bend them to his ambition. So it is in the objective sense that this anti-Rastignac is overcome by *anomie*, a destiny written into his personality, which is meant to be. The Stendhalian hero sees himself surrounded by a Balzacian world, but his personality, too large to be bounded by this world, makes him into an outlaw. The Stendhalian relationship between *anomie* (social) and atypicality (predominantly psychological) is restated more intensely by Dostoyevsky. Stavrogin's spirit forces him to be deliberately violent and contemptuous of the rules and conventions of society. But in James, Conrad, Proust and Joyce, this relationship is drastically modified. Their characters are able to deliver themselves from *anomie* by virtue of an inner life which is expansive enough to mirror the real world, whose rules and conventions are only infringed in their thoughts, or virtually so. It has been said of Virginia Woolf's characters that their sensitivity makes them untypical. The same could be said of the Narrator in *Remembrance of Things Past* or of Broch's *Somnambules* – their sensitivity sets them apart from a world which they observe, and appraise, but always in secret.

This secrecy corresponds to the isolation to which Meredith and James, Proust and Broch, Musil and Kafka all see themselves condemned, all retreating into their own consciousness – i.e., into a cultural world of their own. Throughout the eighteenth century the social world and the world of culture followed parallel courses. As the novel developed its characteristic, recognized form, the novelist acquired a status approximating in esteem to the poet's, the dramatist's or the philosopher's. The worlds of society and of culture were fused in the person of Balzac; just as society needed Bianchon to understand and tend its physical ills, so it had to have a sociological novelist – in this case, Arthez.[21] This conjunction achieved by

Balzac did not last long. In Baudelaire and Flaubert the schism between the life of society and the life of culture is affirmed and consecrated. The language of culture and poetry could no longer be the same as that used by a bourgeoisie preoccupied with establishing its material power, and regarding art as a decorative cover of ideals for its real motives and interest. 'Art for art's sake and business is business are two branches of the same tree' said Broch, commenting on the drama of Hugo von Hofmannsthal, one of the first to denounce the risk of 'reclamation' which the artist ran; everyday speech and the language of poetry had nothing in common, he claimed, but the poet's use of a special language did not prevent the integration of his work into common culture.[22] Poet and novelist were to find themselves as much at odds with their class of origin as with the whole of society, a society which now included an organized and militant working class. If the writer did not choose to copy the language, and hence the values, of the bourgeoisie, nor to yield to aestheticism (which often comes to the same thing), he had to resort to an explicitly subjective language, a language that grew out of his own emotional life, his thought and his own culture. He had to adopt a style which was metaphorical, in the broadest sense of the word, for this was the only way to break the bonds of his objective social situation. The great novelists, from Flaubert on, have had to take for granted the contradiction between cultivated writing and Balzacian reality – a contradiction that is apparent in Virginia Woolf's remark in 1940: 'Take away all that the working class has given to English literature and literature would scarcely suffer; take away all that the cultivated classes have given and English literature would scarcely exist. So cultural education has to play a very important part in a writer's work.'*

What is literature, after Balzac, but, in the first instance, the writer's perception of a radical opposition between reality (social) and truth (human) and at a further remove, the resolution of this conflict through a private world of imagination whose legitimate order will show the contrasting illegitimate and inhuman order of the social world?

It is this situation which constitutes the objective situation confronting the novelist. What he has to do (as he knows only too

* Virginia Woolf, at the W.E.A. conference, Brighton, 1940.

deplorably well) is to depict bits and pieces of a social totality which is not only beyond his grasp, but which has no kind of credible. reality for him. So the novel becomes the art of *transforming* his perception of society into artistic perception even when what he perceives of society for any sensitive and intelligent person is not really worth considering. So the modern novel involves an act of bad faith in a way which has not always been necessary for the novelist. The predominance of bad faith began when literature no longer expresses reality but atones for it – when, in fact, the writer has to try to compensate, by using a language personal to himself, for belonging to an incomplete and one-sided society. He can no longer, like Balzac, portray and criticize a hierarchically ordered society centred on the ruling class, or a state which is virtually identified with it. The *Comédie humaine* was there for Balzac to give utterance to it. Flaubert had to invent a special kind of language which he could not get from 'provincial life'. 'Flaubert', observes Proust, 'had a "style", whereas we cannot really talk of "style" in Balzac.' But Proust did put the word 'style' in inverted commas, to show that Flaubert's writing, since it was appropriate to the subject matter of Flaubert's choice, was just as realistic as Balzac's.

'Emma Bovary, c'est nous'

Appearances do seem to be against Flaubert, who transforms an objective social situation into the language of subjectivity, while the *Comédie humaine* seems to be written directly out of the social situation it presents: real society is not concerned with metaphors – things and people are just what they are.

In his remarkable essay, *Degré zéro de l'écriture*, Barthes makes it clear that Flaubert was the first of the writers who worked so relentlessly at their style because they found it impossible to take up their true social vocation – which is to expose and elucidate social mechanisms and social relationships (like Balzac), instead of (like Flaubert) conveying to the reader his own fascination with things and individuals when they are out of context (if by 'context' is understood the historical situation of a society). 'Style' becomes an alibi enabling the writer to turn aside from his traditional mission as a social-analytical critic of society. By resorting to the kind of strength afforded by colourful imagery, the writer declares his own incapacity to abandon bourgeois reality, which isolates him from the social and political realities of his time as manifested in class relationships and class conflicts.

When one considers *Madame Bovary* purely as a literary product, one can apply this thesis of alienation to its causes – but not to its effects, if Flaubert's mood is perceived in terms of actual social and psychological situations. It seems that Barthes may have refused to recognize that Flaubert's stylistic craftsmanship became essential to the depiction of specific objects. 'Bovarysme', which Girard called the romantic lie, is, after all, an objective reality out of which, to a large extent, a whole series of novels has emerged, from Melville to Conrad, from Dostoyevsky to Proust and from Henry James to Joyce. It was the stage for characters haunted by the hopes, the daydreams and the dreams proferred then by the class to which they belonged – bourgeois or petit bourgeois – while, at the same time, as Lukács has reminded us, their realization was forbidden. This contradiction not ony makes the hero of *Under Western Eyes* or Stephen Daedalus into figures of isolation and rejection along with Emma Bovary; it also renders them guilty. They become the psychological counterpart of the writer's social guilt. How else could Flaubert, who must be regarded as the pioneer, convey the romantic lie of Emma Bovary but through verbal imagery and through comparisons which reproduce her own direct self-presentation and her impulses. There are innumerable people tainted with Bovarysme in societies where the cultural construction of reality, especially through the reading of novels, becomes more and more remote from the social construction of reality proper. Such people are unable to see that this mental imagery hides the actualities of social existence from themselves. They persist in seeing the social world through their imagination, and above all in believing that their imagination can act as intermediary between themselves and the things they desire, things which may be – like Emma's lovers – objects pure and simple, or parts of the social machine. Fundamentally, they are blind to the fact that the world of their imagination is really imaginary. This, of course, is known to the writer who can explain to the reader the experiences which the heroine can only live through. The inner discourse of Emma Bovary, which is the unconscious analogue of Flaubert's psychological discourse, becomes the mode of expression for a sociological reality that is as precise as that depicted by Balzac. The screen obstructing vision has become the instrument of vision.

Flaubert uses 'style' to kill three birds with one stone. First he shows that there is a hidden category of people, whose real value lies in a powerless and anguished subjectivity, and who are lodged within the framework of visible social relationships. Next he shows how Bovarysme (for which society is to some extent responsible, because it evokes unrealizable dreams, which are then taken seriously) isolates these people from real social life and turns them into pariahs. Last, but not least, he demonstrates that the only way of revealing the nature of that life is to show the existence of this gulf between subjective individuality and objective social life with its full array of conventions, rituals and petty rules of precedence – a caricatured reduction of the grand Balzacian apparatus which no longer exists, or which is no longer visible to the writer, at all events.

Yet by making use of a method which consists of moving from the subjective existence of an individual to small-scale social situations (the rural gatherings) and from these to the whole social order the existence of which is only implicit (in reality, there is just a void) he is not merely being as realistic as Balzac. There is no fundamental difference between the method of *Madame Bovary* and that of the *Comédie humaine* so far as the significance of character is concerned. Emma Bovary fails to recognize the part played by her imagination; but Rastignac is not conscious of ambition, nor Runcigen of capitalism. In both cases the writer uses his characters as means of conveying understanding, an understanding which is of the order of myth, in that it represents a *Weltanschauung*, the affirmation of an all-encompassing meaning conferred on human life.

There is, however, a decisive difference between Balzac's characters and those of Flaubert; Balzac's characters – even Pons, who is something of an anticipation of Bovarysme – see themselves as members of society, while Flaubert's characters would like to live as though they were alone, or rather, as though society existed just to enable them to realize their aspirations. Perhaps, on the other hand, there is no difference if one remembers that it was a myth which achieved the transition in fiction from Balzacian society to the social life of Flaubert or Chekhov – the myth of Napoleon. Society, as a coherent order, and as a mechanism (as it seemed early in the eighteenth century) began to disintegrate from the time that Julien Sorel and Fabrice, to begin with, and Raskolnikov later, saw through the superhuman image that was supposed to represent it and which was, in fact, the image of a lost father-figure. Once Napoleon was truly dead it was the Flaubertian design for the novel – an all-embracing subjectivism set over against the constraints of a particular social milieu – which prevailed. It dominated the Western world right up to the 1930s. It is found, mixed with Balzacism, in Gogol and, especially, in the American novels of the 1920s – Sherwood Anderson's *Winesburg, Ohio* and Sinclair Lewis's *Main Street* – in which the generous spirit of one individual is thwarted by the stifling meanness of small-town life.

Yet Flaubert, and James and Proust after him, used 'style' to reverse the Balzacian perspective, in taking as their subject a restricted social scene 'from life' as the immediate context of rather special, perceptive fictional characters whom they elect to serve as receptacles of their own insight. The drawback is that vivid and imaginative description may act as a distorting mirror if there is a disproportionate difference between the objective social situation with which the writer is dealing and his necessarily subjective approach. There is less need in Flaubert's case to stress the consequences for the writer of departing from the 'writing degree zero' than there is in the case of naturalism. If we accept the fact that the emergence of the working class places the writer in an awkward situation from which only 'style' can rescue him, we have also to recognize that resort to 'style' itself leaves the novelist who wants to present society from a working-class rather than a bourgeois standpoint open to misunderstanding.

So, despite the very offensive treatment to which Zola subjected the dominant bourgeoisie and the immense documentary value of what he wrote, *Les Rougon-Macquart* does not do for the working class what *La Comédie humaine* did for the ruling classes. We can, between the lines of Balzac's novel, just discern the system of alienation which Marx was to elucidate later, whereas Zola's novels bear the stamp of what ethnologists nowadays call 'ethnocentrism'. The destitution of the workers, their products, the coal they mine and the engines they drive are clothed in an imagery which belongs to the writer's poetic imagination. Mallarmé's regard for Zola's writing in some ways carries with it a condemnation in social and political terms of the great novelist.

In spite of themselves, naturalistic writers, whose influence continued to predominate up to the First World War, went some way towards vindicating Nietzsche's judgement that art is the last metaphysic available in the midst of European nihilism. Rather than appealing to subjective intuition, they take human misery for their subject so as to shame the bourgeoisie rather than deal with the relevant mechanisms, and social and economic phenomena, of contemporary life. Zola himself certainly thinks in macroscopic terms and is concerned with the basic structure of society; he does, therefore, connect with the constructs and attitudes of truly socialistic thought. Yet other naturalistic novelists fall short of this. Their whole work bears witness to the fact that one cannot simultaneously serve literature and social justice. Heinrich Mann, at least, was aware of this, and we should perhaps regard naturalism in Germany, and to a certain extent in the United States, as directly connected with the principles and ideals of social democracy.[23]

Novelists who detested the bourgeoisie and yet were isolated from other social groups had to seek some other object for their writing, and found it in individualism. Individualism, however, is compatible with two different aspects of the novel, which have too often been confused. With the decline of naturalism, there appeared in fiction a cult of the individual as a unique being holding himself apart from the world and from other people. At the same time, Joyce and Proust developed a conception of the individual in terms of consciousness and of culture; it was this line that was followed by Virginia Woolf, Dos Passos, Broch, Faulkner and Thomas Mann. The idea of the 'bourgeois writer' lacks precision and relevance if one fails to distinguish between these two schools of writers; one in search of uniqueness, the other seeking to express what Proust calls the 'universal mind' – the deep level of understanding common to all men.

At the beginning of this century, particularly in Germany and

Austria, a new fictional genre was born – the *Kunstlerroman* (the novel about the artist) dedicated to the indefinable and special quality of the creative artist enclosed in the ideal world of his art. After the war, the French novel reacted to this cult of the extraordinary by developing a cult of the unique. Giraudoux', Cocteau's and even Cendrars' characters find happiness when they have the feeling that, at a particular time, and in a particular place, they are the only people to be doing some particular thing. But if the German novel (and who knew of Kafka at that time?) firmly rejected social life, it seems to have been an inability to participate in social life which characterizes such novels; i.e. since society does not exist any more, it is better to try to be some kind of unique being than to live out a fragmentary existence.

Interior monologue and industrial society

The 1920s saw the birth and development of two complementary myths – the disintegration of 'society' as an organic whole and the fragmentation of the individual. These two 'threats' were the chosen themes of many critics and essayists who believed that jazz, Cocteau, Freud, Picasso, Proust, Joyce and Pirandello were all pursuing the same ends – the dismemberment of personality, the breakdown of society and the rejection of reality.[24]

The truth is that psychoanalysis and cubism and *Ulysses* did have something in common: they were analytical, but they were analytical in terms of an ultimately holistic conception. They did perhaps enshrine the individual, but not the extraordinary individual.

From 1922 on, one can observe what seems to be one last effort in Western literature to rediscover the wholeness of humanity. History, Daedalus thinks of as nightmare. In negation of history, and its miniature replica, the clock time of industrialism, we find fiction writing patiently worked into elaborate patterns whose form resembles circles rippling out over the surface of a pond after a stone is thrown in. There are precisely defined points of present time which are determinate for the search for a past which could open up the fullness of humanity, a past which offers a refuge from the chronicle of absurdities unfolded in social and political events. The fullness and complexity of myth are rediscovered by these novels, for which *Ulysses* is the model, bridging the gap that separates the gods of the Classical Age from a sleepy middle-class woman in the Dublin of 1904. A similar universal feeling inspires the trilogy of *U.S.A.*, in which Dos Passos sought an American past with some human meaning. The eighteenth-century novel channelled social history into the story of a lifetime. This time, what is combined are an individual's remembrances and the memory of humankind. The interior monologue is a microcosm encapsulating total recall of a liberated span of time, and the novel becomes the meeting point of different psychological and cultural paths.[25]

In the centre of this three-dimensional meeting-place stands the average man (*homme moyen* – who is *sensible*, according to Joyce). Neither ordinary nor extraordinary, standing apart from the masses as from the elite, this new kind of personage is a receptacle, a mirror, a camera. Significantly, Joyce, Mann, Dos Passos, Musil and Kafka select the same human type, a man standing not so much apart, as equidistant between extremes – business and nihilism, the industrialized world and revolution, hope and despair. Musil's and Kafka's heroes pay dearly for their desire to be 'without any distinguishing marks'. Yet at the outset, they do have something in common with Leopold Bloom or Hans Castorp, representing the cultural and humanistic mainstream passing by the turbulence of the modern world and yet enriched by it. This 'average person' exists for the most part in the world of its novel. Sociologically speaking, he is at once valid (there are certain sections of the middle classes which do have easy access to culture) and implausible; for he is all too obviously a simulacrum of the novelist, who infuses him with his own sensibility, his own critical intelligence and his own freely available time and commitment. The primary task of this character is to salve the guilty conscience of the writer, who is both isolated from the working class and detached from the bourgeoisie, or at least from the egoism and inhumanity of the bourgeoisie. When Thomas Mann wants to 'collate' the *Burger* and the *Kunstler* he turns to the humanist and liberal bourgeoisie. The concept of the 'average person' is consonant with Virginia Woolf's observation, quoted earlier – there can be no literature without culture, the workers being 'incapable' of writing literature. But this person plays parts, representing the voluntary ideological and political exile of the writer, recording social life in precise detail, and, in short, affirming the eternal vocation of art.

According to Broch, the mission of the novel is to express not one, but every conceivable *Weltanschauung*.[26] This idea is exemplified in a considerable number of novels set in the more advanced industrial societies. The writer himself stands aside from ideologies, from 'ideas', from class conflicts, because of some overreaching purpose he seems to have in mind of comparing and contrasting them, perhaps of composing their differences. 'Voluntary exile from ideology', in this sense, is itself only too obviously ideological; Musil, like Joyce, seems to have the idea that culture conditions politics. Dos Passos, in the novels he wrote before 1938, shows very little of any sympathy he had for Marxism at the time.[27] Thomas Mann has Hans Castorp adopt 'every kind of *Weltanschauung*', and Joyce's two heroes move about a city which is defined much more in terms of its cultural life than its politics. Broch's *Sleepwalkers* see man being done to death all the time, and in every place, by 'modernism'.

All these novels show an apparent urge to reconstitute some bygone age which possessed more of the completeness and the complexity belonging to human existence. Musil's work is a paradigm – a tragic paradigm – of this posture. *The Man Without Qualities* lives – or rather, slowly dies – in nostalgic longing for the old Austria, which, in 1913, was stifled by the tough-minded pragmatism emanating from Prussia. Indeed, the liberal-mindedness of the old Austrian Empire seems symbolic of most of the values cherished by Wasserman, Thomas Mann, and Dos Passos (in *U.S.A.*): cultural diversity, a sense of proportion, anti-totalitarianism, respect for tradition, distrust of technological progress (all values, be it noted, which Kafka reveals as empty and false). It is an outlook not very different from Freud's philosophy; for him, any cure for the ills of civilization has to begin with self-knowledge, so that man may be delivered from the frustrations, the inhibitions, the lethal repressions which beset him. The past – the past regained – is the logical centre of the human situation.[28]

This kind of fiction would represent liberal conservatism if it were not able, because of its artistic qualities, to give us a realistic as well as critical perception of social existence. The novels of the 1920s display in an exemplary manner the interplay between literature and sociology. The novels of Joyce, Virginia Woolf and Faulkner show that there are necessary relationships between forms in society and forms in art. It is significant that the 1910 Post-Impressionist Exhibition constituted a revelatory turning-point for Virginia Woolf. The paintings seemed to correspond to the new way of writing of which she, like Proust and Joyce, felt the need in order to express new social and psychological realities. It was the same year, 1910, that signalled for her the break-up of the old Victorian order, displaced in favour of shifting, varied, more open social relationships – which she was nevertheless quick to pronounce 'absurd'. In much the same way, Proust, Thomas Mann, Dos Passos and Joyce were inspired by the other arts to try to represent what might be called the more labile condition of contemporary existence, it being understood that the rapid tempo and the complexity of the stream of consciousness and of social relationships are directly and logically related to each other. Realism in the novel attaches to the close relationship between the flexibility of new artistic forms (the treatment of time, in particular, owes much to music) and the no less contemporary sense of the transience of reality. But it is a profoundly critical realism, especially in terms of artistic forms. It is a realism which challenges the social values, and the social apparatus, of a bourgeois civilization.

Other arts were liberated from academicism, and from the moral order it implied, long before the novel (with the possible exception of Henry James' work). But in following the example of the plastic arts, music and the cinema, the novel came some way to validate the demolition of 'Art' carried out by Monet, Picasso and Stravinsky. *Ulysses* and *Jacob's Room* (which it should be remembered, were denounced as 'cubist') and *Manhattan Transfer* too, are accounts, in specifically sociological terms, of the kind of reality which entered into the work of these artists. In Virginia Woolf's first novel, fiction transcends appearances. Dublin is shown minus any moral order. The 'Verdurin clique' is deprived of its masks. Manhattan is revealed in its true light as an ant-heap.

Novelists who refuse to accept a cultural position identical with their position in society eventually discover within the 'social matrix' from which they have come materials which serve as rejections of that matrix. Critics readily endowed this situation – which has specific sociological connotations, with its rapid movement, fleeting figures and disjointed details – with negative meaning. Joyce is said to have reduced human personality to atoms in a degrading fashion; Gide (who, interestingly, 'renounced' the idea of character in his own work) could not bring himself to take any interest in the 'pulverized' creatures in *Manhattan Transfer*. In fact, what we are dealing with is a new *Weltanschauung*, which does certainly imply the individual as parcelled out into fractions, but which also realizes the need to reconstitute individuality properly by projecting these particles of personality patiently and meticulously onto the screen of the conscious mind. Yet, of itself, this whole attitude has neither reality nor meaning. Reality and meaning in this context have to be the products of a whole battery of technical methods, not simply their by-products.

Disintegration as a universal language of discourse

Method, especially in the novel, is never invented by the writer but is a deduction he makes from reality. Since the making of this deduction is in itself a sociological, or at least a social-psychological, process it must be regarded as an integral part of the sociology of the novel. If one goes only by appearances, most of the great contemporary novels are isolated from the real world by their technique and method, which are intentionally made obvious by the writer. But in fact, the various forms of interior monologue, or again, what an American critic has called 'the great structural apparatus of Dos Passos', is the attempt to represent the way in which the currency of moral, religious (and even, in Dos Passos' case, economic) discourse has been disrupted. It is the observable fact of this disruption that the novelist wants the reader to perceive, for without it his work would not have the realism he seeks. The observation itself, however, arises from an intellectual process. If we look at the novels of Joyce and Faulkner, who are especially significant in this connection, their technique can be defined as rendering apparent the difference between the actual experience of destruction and disintegration as a process of thought. It is a process of thought because the writer, unlike the characters he has picked on, is not the recipient, or the register, of the full force of the fleeting, fragmented, incoherent reality, or of the fragmentation of individuals and society which he observes and wants to describe. In order to observe and describe in his writing he makes reference to ideas, to an ideology and even to artistic models which have a coherence and consistency which renders them ludicrously anachronistic. Even if reality did once correspond to that coherent order, what the writer is now observing is a present-day reality made up of scattered contradictory fragments, while 'real' men, particularly those of the middle classes, remain attached, for good or ill, to that self-same system of 'coherently ordered values'. Yet this language of discourse of the past is indispensable to the novelist so he can break it down, reduce it to its elementary fragments. People who accused Joyce and Virginia Woolf of writing chaotic novels came closer to the mark than they knew. They and Dos Passos saw individual beings as isolated, or broken apart from any true social order, much as Braque and Picasso saw objects escaping from the rules of perspective. But in order to create cubism, they had to make *negative* reference to figurative art. The fact that Joyce attacked Thomist thought (and the Catholic church which is a depressing caricature[29] of it) is not really relevant, any more than Faulkner's nostalgia for the social and religious order which he was bound to demolish in literature because he saw it being dismembered in actuality. In both cases the treatment in the novels derives from the breakdown of a metaphysical order, but consciously broken down through the writer's realization that the metaphysical no longer corresponds with reality; the work of artistic disintegration is thus a quite logical process of artistic *creation*. But artistic does not mean 'contrived'. It is dangerous to maintain that the order in terms of which the novel is composed is designed to resolve ideological conflicts in some fictional form or ward off the disorder of bourgeois ideology while the self-same ideology is 'reconstituted' in the novel. One can accept that the modern novel in general provides a fictive solution for the actual social and economic contradictions of the real world; we have dwelt enough on the false problems on which, for example, *The Magic Mountain* is founded – and on its significantly 'open' ending. But as far as the composition of the novel is concerned, whether one is thinking of Mann, or Faulkner, or Joyce or Dos Passos, it seems to us that it develops out of the process of reconstitution and, as a result, no compositional order can be clamped on to a confused ideology in such a way as to make it unconfused. This compositional ordering seems to depend on abstracting from a reality whose essential features are preserved – just as the artistic order of *Guernica* is something abstracted from a particular moment in a war.

Let us take three of the most significant examples – Joyce, Dos Passos and Faulkner. There seems no doubt that the structure of their novels constitutes an artistic – but by no means unfaithful – replication of the disorder of a culture in its ideological as well as its social aspects. In Joyce and Dos Passos the moral order and the social order are taken to pieces, literally before our eyes. And it is even more important to realize that both *Manhattan Transfer* and *Ulysses* have as a framework the confines of a modern city, and as substantive content the activities of that city which, to a sane observer, appear aberrant and inhuman. If we make use – rather unwisely, perhaps – of the terminology of Saussure's linguistics, we could regard the confines of New York City and Dublin in the form of 'signifiers' of an all-inclusive kind (viz. of a world inhumanly 'modern'), and consider that inside the novels we find a complex universe of objects which are what is 'signified' by this all-inclusive 'signifier', but which are also the form – for example, the interior monologue – and not 'contents'. Of course, the novels I have mentioned are the outward manifestation of the individual consciousness or 'subjectivity' which represents perhaps the only *values* deserving the name in industrial societies. It is consciousness of this sort which imposes, or imprints, dislocation and fragmentation on the sequential arrangement of the novel. Nor could it be otherwise, since the 'subjectivity' of the novelist and of his main characters bears on a social reality which is essentially kaleidoscopic in nature. Interestingly, in the plastic arts, this kind of dislocation and fragmentation has a name, 'collage', which has the specific purpose of conveying faithfully the existential and 'ideological' dislocation and fragmentation of the real world. In other words, there is a parallel between the real Dublin and what is picked out from Dublin to serve as literary setting, and a parallel between the discontinuities and disordered life contained within the confines of the city and the discontinuity and disorder – but now exemplary and significant – of the narrative sequence of the book.

Faulkner provides plenty of evidence to support the contention that the structure of a novel may symbolize the actualities of the structure of society without the structure necessarily being an entirely imaginary construct, and without its inherent confusion necessarily being rendered into some kind of order. There is a notable instance of this in one of his stories, 'The Bear', which is about a fabulous beast which represents the legendary past of the South, as does the primeval forest, which has been gradually eaten away by industry and by the railroads and highways. The bear's hunters are a miniature replica of the social hierarchy of the South, interrelated by complex kinship relationships which, as in Homer or in Hesiod, constitute one of the more prominent components of myth.[30]

The death of the bear is clearly symbolic; in killing it the hunters are extinguishing the patriarchal and theocratic order already ended by 'democracy' and its values. *The Bear* gives us not only a striking picture of a social structure, in the strict sense of the term, but also makes no effort to conceal the fact that the two worlds, the old and the new, which now confront each other in the South, are truly *dis*-orders.

These three aspects of the novel – disintegrated reality, disintegrating thought and an aesthetic of disintegration – are in practice indissociable from one another and ought to have given the novel some universal significance. This, at any rate, was the intention – the rather naive intention, perhaps – of those novelists who followed the gospel of a school of painting which, in 1910, still remained the object of abuse. The object in its 'pure state', with its only coherence deriving from 'method', was displayed as a challenge to academicism and the order of bourgeois society, and, at the same time, an appeal addressed to all. Even a politically conservative writer like Faulkner was no longer dealing with the individual character, as he was known in history and in the literary tradition from Marivaux to Tolstoy, nor with the analysis of feelings which had been labelled and codified in novels from *The Princess of Clèves* to *The Charterhouse of Parma*. Instead, he dealt with the notion of psychological and social life perceived in all its immediacy. Such movement did not perhaps represent human life as a whole, as Proust and Joyce imagined. Nevertheless it made some totality seem realizable for human existence in so far as the novel presented objects and people in terms of the analysis of actuality, and not of synthetic abstractions. The aim of art, as a technique of subversion, is to display reality as fragmented, something which orthodox art, in its official capacity, deliberately refused to represent. Once this fragmentary quality has been brought to light and given form, it belongs to the whole of human existence, and no longer to one particular stratum in the social hierarchy. Picasso found the social content that he needed to render into formal truths of universal application in a kitchen, or in a street in Avignon. Joyce, on the contrary, had at his disposal only the bourgeois and petit-bourgeois of Dublin, while Proust had to take Swann and the Guermantes as objects for his art. Yet their novels have, as they were certainly seen to possess when they were written, the same sense of social and artistic affront as Picasso's *Demoiselles d'Avignon*. To read Joyce, or to look at a Klee while thinking in terms of art '*en soi*' and not of 'specific' art, is to fail to see that in both cases objects are represented which, in the artist's mind, are specific to reality by virtue of the very fact that they have been isolated from the apparent and false coherence of 'realism' – i.e. of the institutional order of society. These forms subvert the reality of everyday construction while making actual components of everyday reality transcendently real. The interior monologue abolishes 'society', and discovers social existence.

The myth of 'Metropolis'

There is a striking contrast, in both *Ulysses* and *Manhattan Transfer*, between the atomization of human relationships and the rigid, indeed abstract, terms in which society as a whole is described. The latter is a matter of form in the strict sense of the term. Dublin, New York, Berlin and Vienna are frameworks, confines. It is the city itself, without its citizens, which is the subject. There are very few references to work, or workers' movements, or disturbances. It is only on the last page of *Alexanderplatz*, a novel written in imitation of *Ulysses*, that Albert Döblin's hero takes part in a workers' demonstration. D. H. Lawrence and Jules Romains are the only two novelists of this period who stand out as 'social' writers. Lawrence saw the modern city as the arena for the life-giving struggle between men; Romains sees the city as bringing men together, able to make them realize the possibility of harmonious existence. For other writers, society is inhuman: an anonymous automatism regulates the superficial motions of people, encases their lives and renders them fragmentary. In the preface to the French translation of Döblin's first great novel *Die drei Sprünge des Wang-Lun* (published in 1915 and in every way the antithesis of *Alexanderplatz*) there is a phrase which relates directly to the world-vision of Joyce, Broch and Thomas Mann: 'How can one resolve the problems of a society that has become a formidable machine grinding humanity to dust?'[31]

Leopold Bloom's odyssey takes place in 1904; 1913 is the pivotal year of *The Magic Mountain* and *The Man Without Qualities*, while *Manhattan Transfer* is set in 1924. It was during this period that the myth of technology grew up, with its two faces, the one good, the other evil. It was the second face that obsessed novelists, and their writings were concerned with the real fear of the machine modelling man in its own image. This fear was less strongly felt in the French novel, a fact which indicates the relative industrial backwardness of France in comparison with Anglo-Saxon and German-speaking countries. Yet Proust's world-view is basically akin to that of a writer like Broch; both felt it necessary to strive to defend spontaneity against the stereotype, and human relationships against social conventions.

Thus, to the nightmare of history is added the nightmare of industrial society which takes on the appearance of a clanking robot. Whether or not they had seen Fritz Lang's film, the novelists of the 1920s seem to be haunted by images from *Metropolis*, a film which Musil in his *Man Without Qualities* renders in literary form.[32] In the city of the future, transversed by overhead monorail transport, moving pavements and aeroplane taxis, no one communicates any longer with his fellows, no one has any individuality, or any identity.

The fear that man is nothing more than a police dossier is one of the major themes of the contemporary novel up to Robbe-Grillet and Beckett, who seem to take the same view of the individuality being assimilated into a code number fairly coolly. Yet, what terrifies these novelists is something that ordinary people find reassuring. The possession of an identity card means they are identified as members of society, and therefore have recognized rights. For Joyce's and Dos Passos' characters, on the other hand, once the person has been put into a file he no longer represents a personal history, a true being; he has lost control over his self, his identity.

One possible explanation of the success of detective stories lies in its implicit exploitation of this ambiguity: the criminal has killed or is going to kill; because he is unidentified, he is therefore still free. His punishment is less important to the reader than the discovery of his identity. Everything then falls into plan; order is restored. Since the end of the Second World War, however, the main point of the detective story has no longer been the solving of a mystery but the violence of the struggle between the police and the criminal world in which the police often seem more corrupt than the criminals. In its own way, detective fiction is an expression of the fact that the 'crisis of values' is finished – or rather, forgotten.

The novel, after this period, deals with a truncated universe. It has no place for the life and the struggles of the working class or for the industrial world, with its cosmetic myths of progress and efficiency – which neither Joyce nor Broch (a former industrialist turned writer) would underwrite. It is significant that somebody like Dreiser, who, at the beginning of his career was fascinated by the 'struggle for life', later, in 1925, denounced the myth of 'social advancement' in *An American Tragedy*. The fact remains that the great literary movement of the 1920s confused capitalism with industrialization; it was industrialization, rather than the market economy, which was accused of dehumanizing life.

The 'false myth' of modernity – of an industrial society that is turning life into automation – was challenged by the 'true myth' of the continuous flux of consciousness. But this confrontation implies a contradiction, since the purpose of the interior monologue was to exorcise the very forces to which it owed its existence. Modern life, deafening, artificial, flattening, has not only revealed to men the preciousness of inner life; its pressure has also tapped the source of the stream of consciousness. *Manhattan Transfer* is important because its characters, reduced by the city to a mechanical existence, are trying to salvage some odds and ends of their memories and their personal life. Itis the city that forces them somehow or other to retreat into that interior monologue which we find Leopold Bloom exploiting fully and in which he recaptures – by breaking it down into its constituent parts – a whole universe. In one sense the interior monologue contributes to the oppressive forces from which it seeks to escape, in another, if resort to the 'stream of consciousness' does allow the individual to find himself, it condemns him to be a per-petual recorder of life, and thus to passivity and restlessness. This contradiction explains the breadth and the remarkable thematic unity of 'subjective' fiction – and also explains its short duration. Until about 1930, the crisis in Western civilization (which had been the determining influence in fiction since the end of the preceding century) had passed through two stages – one characterized by individualism, the other by its dedication to a combination of recollection and consciousness, which passively received and recorded what was happening in the world at large and re-created its own cultural world. From the 1930s on (although Broch continued to write and Musil was gradually moving the 'man without qualities' on towards the nothingness of his end) the 'crisis of values' really becomes something meaningful. For Malraux and Bernanos especi-ally, the question was how to resolve the 'crisis' by making a 'life of values' accessible, here and now, and for everyone. This particular move, which historically spells the return of the novel to linear narrative, came to nothing in the end, just as the interior monologue of Joyce was of no avail against the prevailing indifference of the time.

Myth still essentially reflects historical reality, but the novel has come to represent different kinds of experience within this comple-mentary manifestation of experience. During the 1930s the myth of death began to dominate fiction; the liberal humanism of *The Magic Mountain* was shattered by social and political realities of a kind too familiar to recite here. Malraux's characters were offered up as sacrifices to this humanism – and to its antithesis, the praxis of revolution. It may be, however, that the sublimation of death which we find in Hemingway, Malraux, Lowry, Fitzgerald and Bernanos is only the reflection of death in terms of society; we find, in the West, concern with this sort of death replacing conflict, at best uncertain, between the bourgeoisie and the working class. It is no accident that the novel became peopled with characters who have nothing to do with the ruling classes (any more than with the trade union movement or with any revolutionary struggle) and who are at the same time indifferent to culture – barmen, errand boys, clerks, pimps, detectives, hawkers and 'marginal men'. The hero, in this new 'social realism'[33] has no regard either for culture or for introspection; his only need is to survive and, if he can, to find love. Roquentin, in *La Nausée*, thinks the past a luxury for the propertied classes. If one added death as well, Roquentin might be the reference point for the characters of Céline, Graham Greene, Carson McCullers or Elizabeth Bowen. Roquentin, we feel, brings to light the latent myth of the absurdity of existence, and makes it a solid starting point from which action can open up the road to liberty.

Kafka without fear

It is, however, Kafka's writings which attain the widest and most relevant sociological significance. His novels deal with the essential structure of society, together with the nature of social change, from the beginning of this century until the present, if the assumption is made that Western civilization has not undergone any really radical social revolution. Kafka wrote during the same period as Joyce and, a little later, Virginia Woolf, Broch and Musil. Yet it is their conception of personality that he arraigns and, finally, condemns – the immense efforts made in *A la recherche* and *Ulysses* to find salvation for man by stretching consciousness to the full. In social status, sensitivity and intelligence, the bank clerk in *The Trial* resembles Leopold Bloom and Quentin Compson in *The Sound and the Fury*. But unlike Quentin, 'K' does not break his watch in an attempt to abolish socially defined time; he has grasped that society's time is essentially his own time, and that the individual is already a dead man if he cannot read the time by the clock to which judges, juries and barristers work.

To search for time which is lost and gone (*la recherche du temps perdu*) is futile when society is itself lost, when the individual can no longer recognize himself in it, and when society regards individuals as anonymous social units, rigorously ordered in an anonymous whole. The main fictional characters of the 1920s all move around in circles, but while to Bloom and Daedalus these journeys are involuted – the more they move about the city the more they turn in on themselves – K. executes his circle in a blind social system, telling himself, with unassailable logic, that he will have no existence if he is lost sight of – unless he too allows himself to become blind. Kafka's hero inverts the myth of that king of ancient Greece who (in that same Austria where the young Jewish writer felt himself to be free and imprisoned) so fascinated Freud. Oedipus blinds himself in an effort to destroy the trap in which the gods have caught him, so that he can then gain recognition from the city. K., on the contrary, wants to gain recognition from men, and looks everywhere in society, until that society closes his eyes and thus gets rid of an intruder who reproaches it, as Oedipus reproached the gods, for depriving him of his being. It is because of the extra eye which both the Greek king and the bank clerk of Prague possess,* that they know where oppression lies and where salvation may be found.

Kafka's work, which has something in common with *Hamlet* and *The Brothers Karamazov*, brings within the same rigorous structure three forms of the human condition – the metaphysical, the psychological and the social. There is a passage in *Wedding Preparations in the Country* that seems to be central to his view of society; the narrator in great anguish of spirit realizes that his 'I ...' should really be construed in the third person: 'One ...'[34] So the heroes of *America*, *The Trial* and *The Castle* come to believe that this 'one' must be, or must once again become, personal, otherwise only death

*cf. A. Green, *Un Oeil en trop*, Paris, 1969. (The title is taken from a line in Hölderlin: 'King Oedipus, perhaps, had one eye too many.')

remains. The hero of *Metamorphosis* can be said to forestall death by turning himself into an insect-object. The central theme of Kafka's novels is not the way in which the modern world depersonalizes humanity, but much more an hypothesis which is verified – by a negative result, as in a trial – by the hero's journey into oblivion.

This radical transition from the personal to the impersonal (and vice versa) signifies the death of civilization, of culture and of humanity. There is, between *Ulysses* and *The Trial*, a difference similar to that which separates mechanical compliance from unconscious submission. Instead of the mythical and symbolic theme of mechanization which Joyce, Broch and Musil use to designate modern society, Kafka has the machine of *In the Penal Settlement*: man lives in a state of mortal anonymity which is systematically branded on him. Bloom–Ulysses and Daedalus–Telemachus rediscover themselves at the end of an immense interior monologue in the course of which culture, its only truth, is plucked out of the real world; some time later, the clown of *City Lights* slips between the cogs of the machine unscathed, to set out on roads that always lead somewhere else. Kafka's man only succeeds in becoming what he refuses to be – a machine for living.

Lukács clearly perceived the meaning of this assimilation of the human particle into the social whole. He preferred Thomas Mann to Kafka because, in *The Magic Mountain*, the crisis of values does at least remain an open question, while *The Trial* eliminates the very possibility of such a crisis. But Lenin might have preferred the Prague bank clerk to the Castorp of *The Magic Mountain* with his testimony about the verbal struggle of 'progressivism' and 'revolution'; for he would have seen how in Kafka contemporary civilization has reduced man to an object, and stripped the word 'value' of any meaning.

There is a Kafka myth, just as there was a Rimbaud myth. Kafka's stories were supposed to represent blueprints for a bureaucratized, labyrinthine concentration-camp world made up of waiting-rooms and of corridors leading eventually to the police station or the torture chamber. This leaves completely out of account how tenaciously Kafka's heroes strive to have their own individuality, their own reason – and thus, individuality and reason *per se* – acknowledged. If, at the end of *The Trial* and *The Castle* we perceive the shapes of these anonymous, absurd and omnipresent forces with which contemporary history is peopled, the content of the story is none the less made up of a quest which political totalitarianism would make utterly impossible. This quest, tragic and ridiculous though it may be, takes place in a world that Kafka knows by sight, as Broch and Musil have seen it. It is free but departmentalized, anarchic but over-organized, with no common ground between the intentions of the 'I' and the laws of the unidentified 'third person singular' epitomized by the State. Following Nietzsche, Kafka put liberalism on trial: on the one hand there is the apparent freedom of the individual, on the other, the structure of the totality. The concept of the absurd, as it occurs in Kafka's novels, does not belong to the absolute power of the rationality of the State over individuals, but to the lack of communication between them. Any-one may knock on the doors of administrative power, but behind these doors the officials speak a generalizing, legalistic language so that the replies they provide for the individual inquirer always concern his type of situation, never his individual case. The in-dividual's mistake is to believe that there is any consonance between his own reason and the logic of the representatives of power. What Kafka, like Musil, observed was a social organization in which bureaucracy, originally conceived as a means of providing liberty with the rule of law, became an organism with its own *raison d'être* and its own identity. Kafka's novels reveal not so much the terrifying absurdity of the human condition, as more simply and more cruelly, a new status for the person – that assumed by every citizen of Berlin or of Dublin as soon as he has anything to do with an organ of the State. In a totalitarian country the police come one morning, arrest you and throw you in jail, then a trial is arranged. In the liberal State, the essential point is that justice takes its course. What K. wants is to deflect this course improperly by involving himself in a counter-inquiry. The two men who come at the end of *The Trial* to seize K. do not kill him; they put him out of the way because his obsessive desire to know what is happening makes him socially beyond redemption. The example he sets is dangerous; one must never get in touch with the State before it gives you the signal to do so. Agreed, the State is an absurdity, but this absurdity does not seem to have the terrifying meaning that so many critics have given it.

Its absurdity depends on the fact that instead of being ordered, as K. imagines it to be, it is prey to confusion and disorder. When he does eventually manage to telephone the authorities, the Surveyor is overwhelmed by a mad cacophony of sound.

This deceitful and cacophonous order is characteristic – a symbol – of the whole of society. It is what Joyce's heroes, and Jimmy Herf the journalist in *Manhattan Transfer*, perceive and want to escape from. They do not want to be like the central figures in the two most sociologically significant American novels of the 1920s – Sinclair Lewis's *Babbitt* and James Farrell's *Studs Lonigan*. Babbitt ends up by seeing that what he had thought of as his own individual life has been controlled by a social machinery, while Studs Lonigan sees himself in the way the cinema has taught him to see himself: 'in pictures'.

Kafka, however, does not merely compel the reader of Joyce to regard the reality of his existence as 'socialized' into absurdity. His work can be seen as even more relevant to our own times than to the period of the 'crisis of values'. Virtually unknown until 1945, his novels have suffered the fate of all myths – of being subject to interpretation. Because of Kafka, the idea of the 'absurd' designates a specific account of social relationships and of relationships between the individual and authority – in short, of the situation of the individual – characterized by anonymity, automatism and lack of responsibility. With this schema as point of departure, the novel seems, however, to have committed itself in two very different directions. The first projects Kafka's world into the future and has a kind of exorcising function, while the other is followed by writers who provide their characters with an ethic and a mode of conduct which are adapted to the kind of reality outlined by Kafka. Novelists who follow the first direction present a totalitarian society where individuals, all formed in the same model, are never free from the inspection and the sanctions of authority. Those who follow the other direction are more careful and more realistic. They seem to set their characters on Kafka's road without allowing it to end in death. *Le Voyeur*, *Molloy* and *The Planetarium* portray social life as a game of chess in which, however, pieces are not under the remote control of an authority which is totally blind. If the pieces in this game are interchangeable, or virtually so, the novels do, nevertheless, include a central character who demonstrates that in life the important thing is not to get caught (Robbe-Grillet), that life is only interesting because of the numerous combinations obtainable with the same elements (Beckett) or, finally, that to live means searching for the 'other', the outline of whose appearance is perhaps visible, but whose personality can never be discerned (Nathalie Sarraute). What we learn from these novels is that society is neither good nor bad; the question is – and this sends the reader back to the problem Lukács posed – whether society and men are real, or whether they are conventional, absurd fabrications?

The phantom society

The basic theme of present-day fiction in its most original forms is clearly that society is too remote from the individual for him to have any sense of being a social identity. It is a theme which serves to promote the ideology of a dominant class, but we have already made clear the dangers of accepting this kind of over-simplified explanation of critical fiction. It is, in any case, clear that the remark by one critical essayist: 'the novel is the private experience of society',[35] has been confirmed to an ever greater extent since 1945. What one might call an infra-sociology characterizes the novel from Queneau to Nathalie Sarraute, from Carson McCullers to Malamud and from Vian to Salinger. As a corollary, fiction has become less and less didactic. The *Bildungsroman* is dead. The novelists who might be called 'cultural' do not put society on show to their readers; they teach them to dodge it, to slip through its net. Yet at the same time these novelists focus on specific milieux and on human relationships meticulously described. No Babbitts, no K.s – which may perhaps explain the popularity of Salinger and Saul Bellow in the United States. One of the important keys to the contemporary novel is the social trickery which characters (Herzog, for example) practise in their endeavours to protect their sensibility, their reason and their dreams from a society whose 'grossness' (as Proust put it) and acquisitive fever they regard with irony, without being particularly shocked. Balzac's kind of sociology can be found today in a new genre – the documentary novel, with which we shall deal by way of conclusion. As for best-selling novelists, they are equally unwilling to take present-day society as their subject, even in their trilogies and huge panoramic narratives.

Saul Bellow has observed[36] (and here Robbe-Grillet and Beckett are in agreement) that the novelist has been deprived of that tragic sense of life that Unamuno made so much of, and which was felt by both Heinrich and Thomas Mann, Dos Passos, Musil and Kafka as much as by the novelists of the 'Beat Generation', among whom was the most penetrating psychological novelist of the twentieth century, Scott Fitzgerald. The 'terrible machine that grinds human bodies to dust', which had made too much noise before the Second World War not to conceal the kind of life the working classes led, is now silent, so far as the novel is concerned. The novelist no longer seems to hear the racket that the land surveyor in *The Castle* makes when his vain search for a coherent and humane world is ended. Between *Manhattan Transfer* and *Molloy* and between *Les Chemins de la liberté* and *Le Voyeur*, one can see the same distinction that MacLuhan draws between the 'hot' civilization of the past and the 'cool' civilization of the presnt.[37] The cool novel is comparable to kinetic art and electronic music, and arouses much the same kind of discussion about the destination of art in bourgeois society.

This silence – this time the silence of infinite space – about the situation of society belongs also to science fiction, in which present-day society is forgotten, projected entirely into the future – 'entirely', since most of these stories arise from the hypothesis that technology, transcending social and ideological struggles, has realized the unity of mankind which has now only to subdue, or be subdued by, extra-terrestrial forces. Jules Verne may be the father of science-fiction, but we would nominate Kafka as its godfather. Science-fiction seems to offer two contrasting interpretations of the one-dimensional world of *The Trial*. Either this world, transported to the planets, carries within itself its own damnation for having surrendered to the machine and forgetting human values, or else, by reason of standardization itself, it achieves a happy, superhuman condition in which it is possible for all man's desires to be satisfied – including his desire for heroics, since the cosmos is also made up of evil forces which have to be subjugated. Science-fiction has in it something of a contemporary philosophy of leisure, and, moreover, is perhaps better able than other fictional forms to fulfil what has been the mission assumed by the novel from *Don Quixote* to *Ulysses*: of elevating historical and social experience into myth.

The field of social realism in the novel has rapidly shrunk as human life has become more and more defined in society's terms, and social groups have become larger and more differentiated. This is no paradox since, in order to describe social phenomena, it is necessary not only for the writer to be able to observe them but also for their structures, their different levels and their processes to be observable. Social differentiation is brought about as a direct result of the increased mass of social groups. Human life has become divided into highly specialized zones of production; men are caught up in a network of information, images and sounds. So-called modern societies are fond of idols, and of 'personalizing' political power, but they only recognize themselves in terms of milieux, sectors, strata and masses. These societies, in accordance with the wishes of the dominant milieu, accept the semblance of homogeneity for themselves. If Balzac were alive today, he would still find servants, old maids and madmen, but without their distinctive garments. Above all, these social samples would convey no social meaning to him through what they said. They would speak a uniform language, made up of projections and identifications, regulated in terms of audio-visual media, the press and the motor car. The durable 'type' has been killed off by the ephemeral 'case'. A man cannot achieve recognition for what he is, which is the subject of Ellison's novel, *The Invisible Man*. The truly realistic novelists of today are sociologists; to get to understand men it is no longer enough to listen to them – they must be questioned.

When a society is inclined to forget what it really is, this forgetfulness is reflected through art, and especially through literature, experimental or not. There is no question but that the novel is undergoing a backlash from two tendencies, more or less latent, which have divided the Western world for the last twenty years or so. Some believe, declare and hope that they can achieve a progressive elimination of social problems, class conflicts and polital ideologies.

Others look to the future for the fully socialized man. This Mani-
cheean situation (as those who follow the former tendency are
pleased to call it) has contributed to the appearance of groups and
individuals who are not merely a-social, but actually anti-social.
They are, or have been, manifest in the Living Theatre group, the
underground cinema, and forms of fiction which, to some extent,
offer in violence a response to the cold playfulness of the 'nouveau
roman' – which does not, it must be remembered, belong exclusively
to France. The idea of a counter-society, and the actual existence of
counter-social groups, was present in the novels of Jack Kerouac
and exists now in William Burroughs. In their stories there are
hallucinations, desires and actual living pleasures, while fictional
eroticisms, both sanctified and systematized, are deployed as manifestations of conformism and products of the mass media. It is
quite possible and justifiable to speak of a revival of the picaresque –
violence, corrosive criticism and a caustic attitude are just as much in
evidence among 'characters' when order is too well established as it
is when order is yet to be established. [38]

Myth is always an integral part of fiction. But the truth about a
society manifests itself through the nature of its social relationships.
The ideological status of our society must be sought in the conformist
novel, if by conformism we mean the comfortable tradition of
Balzac, Stendhal, Céline or Proust. But the meaning of our society
and its value is always brought out by the *franc-tireurs* of institutional fiction, whether they ignore or despise what is 'social'.

CHAPTER 4

The Reading of Fiction

TOGETHER with the cinema, the novel is the narrative mode that responds, or corresponds, most closely to our conventional psychological processes and modes of behaviour. Madame de La Fayette, Stendhal and Proust have, one after the other, taught us to understand the changes undergone by feelings of jealousy. We can follow the evolution of the concept of personality, of our perception of time, through eight centuries of the novel's development. Fiction rationalizes the imaginary, short of asserting its superiority over logic. It can turn a historical and social situation into myth, or, on the other hand, take on the iconoclastic role of demolishing mystery. All the facts of civilization, culture and politics regularly become material for novels. Even surrealism has had its life prolonged in fiction. Yesterday it was the achievements and methods of psychoanalysis which were imported into the novel; today, it is the turn of structural linguistics.

In one respect, however, there is a radical distinction between the novel and the theatre, together with, in part, the cinema; the distinction is functional – the sacred. The novel sets out and develops the relationship existing between the truth of myth and historical reality, while drama imposes significance of a metaphysical kind on historical reality. As Lukács has emphasized, the tendency of the novel is to combine myth with history in order to produce the semblance of man in his entirety. This at least seems to have been its purpose until the time of the Second World War. Drama, on the contrary, expresses what man may dare, or fear, as a function of his historical situation. It is the nature of drama to present man as the challenger, fortunate or unfortunate, of history. He cannot, on pain of death, allow himself to be snared by historical determinism; he must either repudiate it or overcome it. *Antigone, Richard II, Lorenzaccio, Le Prince de Hambourg, Tête d'or* and the plays of Brecht express in many different and contradictory ways the same moral – that the world of values, whether they concern heroism or the will, cannot be the result of historical development. Creon is compelled to admit that Antigone is in the right: political duty, however ineluctable, must give way to religious necessity, if it is not to become valueless. Richard II's transgression of the principle of legitimacy must lead him to his downfall. Again, Lorenzaccio and the Prince of Hamburg demonstrate the fact that history cannot be an end in itself, while Claudel and Brecht, in an industrial society, insisted that man could not be reduced to a mere historical factor.

We must also note how far removed is the novel, in period after period, from tragedy and from other forms of drama. Both *Faust* plays are at odds with *Wilhelm Meister*. *Don Quixote* can be contrasted with *Life is a Dream*, the picaresque novel with the plays of Corneille, Racine and Molière, Stendhal with *Hernani, Lorenzaccio* and *Chatterton*. Again, Strindberg's terrifying plays, from which the whole expressionist theatre derived, can be set against the naturalism of the period. Proust on the one hand, Claudel on the other; Dos Passos as against O'Neil; Thomas Mann as against Brecht.

To write a novel or to read one is to put one's trust in time. But, in drama, time is never a value.

Yet, in spite of this distance between the novel and drama, a closer relationship between the two can be observed in the case of Dostoyevsky and Kafka who, like the tragic dramatists, deny the historical nature of man. At the present time, too, the two modes seem to have moved closer together; novels and plays are often linked by the idea of the absurd, which, as we have seen, conceals a kind of rejection or ignorance of the situation of society.

Reading a novel is usually a solitary activity, in no sense tragic, situationally bound up with the book itself, whose physical make-up often influences the response of the reader. Novel reading is, moreover, very much a matter of culture and ideology, which implies a fundamental confusion between the novel and literature. It is not surprising that the dividing line between the sociology of the novel and the sociology of literature as a whole should be so hard to draw, since the novel is itself the foundation of literature. It is with a novel that a writer makes his debut, and publishers, anxious not to frighten off the public, continue to describe as novels writing of a kind which is scarcely narrative, of a kind which Forster would have found disconcerting. Publishers, moreover, list novels, poems and essays under the heading of 'general literature'. In France in 1967, there were 7,140 titles under this heading, of which 3,125, or 37 per cent, were reprints.[1] But if one consults the catalogues of leading publishers (excluding those that specialize in detective stories, thrillers or science fiction) one finds that at least 70 per cent of the books that fall into the category of 'general literature' are novels. Yet the number of novels produced hardly corresponds to their share in the book market, for out of ten published novels seven will not sell more than 2,000 copies, two will reach a figure between 10,000 and 20,000 and one, going above 20,000, will reach the best-seller class.

These facts are not cited merely in connection with the fact that in France, in 1967, 57 per cent of the population did not read any books.[2] The number of novels produced, which seems at once sizeable and small, is bound up with what, following Roland Barthes, can be called the institutionalization of fiction. A publishing company houses an editorial staff made up of the managing editor and an editorial establishment. They pronounce on a manuscript after consulting reports sent in by readers – often 'outside' readers. A novelist who wants to get published has to break through several barriers. If he is just starting, he knows, or thinks he knows, that he will have more chance of getting published by one particular publisher than by another. But the law of competition, the size of the market and the attraction of literary prizes have created a situation in which no kind of novelist is ever 'blacked' and books of each and every kind of talent get into print. But does the notion of talent measure up to any worthwhile objective criteria? The law, perhaps the myth, of 'good French', whether the model be Gide or Céline, enjoys an undisputed supremacy. There are many novels that remain unpublished because they are 'in bad French'. The 'primitive' writer seems to have less chance than the 'primitive' painter. The laws about 'writing' are in fact closely tied up with those of the market. Between 1958 and 1963, Françoise Sagan's success encouraged publishers to bring out a number of novels by very young writers, in the hope that some amongst them would meet with the same good fortune.

Publishing is selective, but criticism is even more so. A reviewing market, or even what one might call a reviewing lottery, undeniably exists. When the literary prize season opens in France, critics have to deal with a spate of fiction which they can hardly cope with; the criteria by which they decide to devote an article to a particular writer are varied and unreliable. It is the duty of the press officer of a publishing house to get the largest possible number of reviews for each author being published. He will, however, concentrate his efforts on the writer who has been read favourably by the most influential critic. It may then be possible to set machinery going capable of sweeping the author to fame. But the machinery also carries the novelist onto a particular stylistic track from which he is not expected to deviate. The question is whether he will 'fulfil his promise'. This is the question for the publisher and the critic who have both invested – in terms of money and prestige – in the new novelist.

We do not apply any value judgement to this method of producing novels, which is much the same in all Western countries. All it means is that it has to be remembered that it is this organization which determines the readership of fiction. It is even possible to speak of 'over-determination', if one takes into account the circulation figures of the mass newspapers and the impact of radio and television. Apart from those who are particularly well-educated and really interested in literature, no one chooses for himself the novel he is going to read.

The reading of fiction is also subject to sizeable changes in terms of the time and the place reading happens. Laclos' novel, *Les Liaisons dangereuses*, must be entirely different today (even if one forgets about the film, *Les Liaisons dangereuses*, 1960) from what it was when published in 1782.[3] What attracts readers today is the mechanics – the 'action' – rather than the realism or the moral of the novel. The action, however, is of some consequence to the frame of mind of the reader. *Les Liaisons dangereuses* provides a model of licentiousness for social milieux inclined nowadays to turn away from Sartre's tragic social realism and look for the melodramatic, wry, gallantries found in, say, the kind of thing produced by *nouvelle vague* films over a number of years. As we remarked earlier, reading Stendhal – and writing like Stendhal – after 1950 symbolized a rejection of everything that was summed up in *La Nausée*, *Les Chemins de la Liberté*, the realist Italian cinema and Marxism in general. At the very time when many French intellectuals were becoming enthusiastic about Faulkner, the American intelligentsia preferred Gide and Camus – regarding Faulkner as 'too tough and violent'. Yet, at the same time, the position of Saint-Exupéry remained remarkably secure. Combining, in a delicate and lucid style of writing, the worlds of adventure, heroism and universal humanism – (the aeroplane crossing frontiers and the pilot looking down on the earth from on high), he became as popular in the Soviet Union as in France. The bourgeoisie of the 1930s read *Le Grand Meaulnes* for reasons that cannot have been in Alain Fournier's mind; *Le Grand Meaulnes* represented a breath of pure and dreamlike air amidst the 'harsh realities of life'. Detective stories have two kinds of readers. For the great majority they provide escape, a refuge, a pastime; there is a fairly clear cultural distinction which separates detective stories, thrillers and spy stories from other literature; they are read because they offer distraction. Yet they are also read by many intellectuals as a kind of game, as recreation; the subject of the story interests them less than the working out of the plot and the highly coloured language.[4] These novels are also of great documentary interest. Apparently, a more exact account of American society is to be found in the stories translated in the Série Noire publications than in the novels of Saul Bellow.

A considerable development has taken place, particularly in France, in the sociology of reading and the sociology of writers, and interesting results are beginning to appear.* However, although we are learning more and more about 'who reads what', how a book circulates in different milieux and what a particular public is prepared to read, the same studies also show how far reading is still regarded as a vice, severely sanctioned in so-called advanced

*Especially noteworthy is the work of the Institut de Littérature et de Techniques Artistiques at Bordeaux directed by Roger Escarpit, in which researchers with different interests are grouped together; through their efforts the whole picture of reading habits in France is beginning to be filled in.

societies. Freedom to read is both encouraged and discouraged. There is little time to read because of the demands made by work and the distractions of cinema, radio and television and the car, while, at the same time, Dostoyevsky's novels have never been so accessible and cheap. The public is kept well informed about experimental and revolutionary forms of art, yet, at the same time, the whole machinery of production mentioned above hinders their diffusion. Municipal or specialized libraries are the public museums of literature, yet access to *avant-garde* work in these libraries is controlled by what can only be called class privilege.

It is no secret that people with higher or even average education regard experimental and revolutionary works as a badge of intellectualism and snobbery; so the resistance of both white-collar and blue-collar workers to Joyce is hardly surprising, not only because *Ulysses* seems impossibly far removed from them but because novels which gain immediate acceptance in middle-class milieux are so much more readily available. But, although this situation has not really changed, it has to some extent been modified in the last twenty years. 'Masterpieces' are integrated into the culture and find their place in syllabuses for students much more quickly than in 1940 (André Breton appears in the 1970–71 Aggrégation syllabus) and information about new work hot from the press is much more quickly distributed.

But the sheer efficiency of this information service and of the distribution of cultural artefacts tends to conceal the existence of a rigid cultural hierarchy, a positive secrecy surrounding culture and knowledge. In 1962–3 an interesting piece of research was carried out on 4,716 recruits to the armed forces. They were divided into five categories according to their educational level (uncompleted primary education; junior high school certificate; uncompleted secondary education; baccalaureate (secondary school certificate); higher education). The recruits were asked to name five authors they knew. The results showed that there was a great difference between knowing the name of an author and reading his work, and also that social class had a definite bearing on 'knowledge' of a writer. Thus, the name of Saint-Exupéry was known to all, while only the 'students' named Maurois, Bazin and Montherlant. Camus, Hemingway and Sartre 'start' from the level of secondary education upwards, while

Dumas was 'abandoned' by those who had gone beyond the baccalaureate; Bruce disappeared after the level of uncompleted secondary education.[5]

My own interpretation (which is admittedly highly debatable) of these findings is as follows: J. Bruce had certainly been read in the lowest two categories, just as Sartre, Malraux, Bassin, Gide and Montherlant had been read in the highest; the presence of Sartre in the category of 'uncompleted secondary education' is only explained by the existence of contemporary mechanisms of information, or by school policy. The reading of Saint-Exupéry is due especially to the popularity of *The Little Prince* and to the ideology which surrounds this writer as a person. In any case, it strikes me as significant that none of the following writers were mentioned at all: Faulkner, Dostoyevsky, Proust, Céline, Bernanos, Robbe-Grillet.

How is the novel, or fiction as a whole, regarded? The answer to this question was the object of an investigation I undertook at the University of Antony in 1965, among 280 people in four occupational categories. The sample was naturally too small to produce significant results, but some findings of this research can be added to the dossier on the sociology of the novel.

What I wanted to do to begin with was to distinguish reading a novel from reading other kinds of literature in terms of the conditions under which it took place, and of comprehension. I wanted, secondly, to find out which novels had been read and what sort of impression the reader retained, and lastly to find the social and cultural significance of fiction and the novel as works of art.

As might be expected, for those in categories *C* and *D* (white-collar and blue-collar workers) the last novel read was often a detective or spy story, while the only Butor mentioned had been read by one woman in category *A* ('liberal professions and teachers'). The same divergence in taste appeared when we asked our informants to mention other novels that they remembered. More interesting is the fact that neither the cinema nor television seemed to interfere with reading novels; those who saw the most films were also those who read the most novels. However, the choice of film seemed less determined by occupational status than the choice of a novel. Going to the cinema on a particular day seems to be customary leisure activity – a form of entertainment; but in choosing a novel, social and cultural barriers intervene. The same person who reads strip cartoon stories may well have been to see *The Wages of Fear* and *Rebecca*. I found also that in choosing a particular kind of entertainment, and especially in choosing a novel, the subject matter had less influence than the way in which a person comes across it. One young worker had been reading nothing but Dostoyevsky ever since he left school because his mother had given him the complete works. Many subjects read only condensed novels that they get every month and others only the novels sent to them by a book club. It was odd to find that the replies to the question 'Have you read more since paperbacks came in?' were, for the most part, negative, which suggests something of a contradiction. The analysis of the questionnaire makes it clear that paperbacks are frequently read, and we have outside evidence of the ambiguous effect paperbacks have on reading. The Livre de Poche series put *La Nausée* and *L'Affaire Mauritius* within reach of everyone, although such novels may well have been submerged in a tide of fiction of all kinds which neutralize each other.

In general, fiction seems to be perceived as a single category. Some respondents in category *A* stressed their interest in certain aspects – action, plot, setting or characterization. Yet respondents in category *A* and in category *B* (middle management and small business men) seemed more interested in the fate of the hero than in the story as a whole. The opposite view was found in categories *C* and *D*. We were also able to collect interesting information concerning readers' identification with particular characters. The only respondent who made any clear identification with the hero of a novel was a retired middle-aged manager, a very peaceable man – and his hero was Raskolnikov! The intellectuals in category *A* all denied identifying with a character; in fact, the problem of identification was something they had thought about. Also, in the majority of cases people are on guard against the glamour of a hero and against anything romantic. They identify with Julian Sorel or Jean Valjean when they are young. Nevertheless, characters had a much more real existence for those in categories *A* and *B* than for those in *C* and *D*; the former would compare a character with a 'real person'; to the other two, especially *D*, characters seemed, as a rule, unreal and remote.

Thus, the further down the social scale one goes, the more the novel is regarded as entertainment, or as a form of escape. In category *A* people seem to want the novel to be true to life, or at least plausible, and the characters to have some psychological or social interest. Those in category *B* wanted to see the character as a model of efficiency, of humanity, of goodness – 'the great physician', for example. *A* readers did not worry about whether or not the novel was shocking, but in the other categories there was a growing concern to read only 'decent' novels. A more important point is that 'educated' readers wanted the novel to deal with contemporary social and political problems. In this respect the result of our inquiry can be correlated with the results of a study made by I.L.T.A.M. which suggested the titles of imaginary novels to a variety of occupational categories. Engineers, technicians, teachers and students all chose *Men on Strike*, rather than *Green Meadows* or *Boulevard of Sorrow*.

The results of this investigation led us to put the problem of working-class reading in these terms: if people do read novels it is not to find out about life or the real world in them. Out of the seventy working-class men and women in the sample, twenty-four never read novels, or at least had not read them for many years. Most of the others, when they read novels, looked for entertainment, escape, or what amounted to sublimation – but all expressed in realistic and consistent terms. Yet one must emphasize the ambiguity that emerges from comments on 'the last novel you read', or 'novels you remember'. The novel is expected to entertain, not because it ought to be but because there is nothing else it can do. From a working-class point of view, the novel is a mythical creation, a source of illusion, with which it is possible to make contact, but in which it is inconceivable to look for 'reality'.

Yet many of them did recognize, in the course of interviewing, that they had derived a great deal of pleasure from reading some novel which reminded them of some war-time experience or, perhaps more often, something connected with their job. Working-class people seem to have a deep desire to read – if only they had time – novels that deal with the actual conditions of life as they know them. It can hardly be necessary to spell out the degree of alienation that this wish implies, seeing that the worker, with no literary education and regarding 'great literature' as inaccessible, longs to be brought in touch with the realities of everyday life – which are themselves alienating. The lower the social and occupational level, the wider the divergence between culture and reading. For the 'liberal professions' culture means books, plays and works of art. For technicians and business-men, culture has a more marked occupational relevance and novels are despised. For clerical workers, there is an unbridgeable gulf between their own experience of life and the novel, while manual workers, for whom culture is an essentially technical or practical affair, can only regard fiction as something of an abstraction, which might be pleasurable. In all these cases, culture must be defined first and foremost as what one knows about.

The results gained from this investigation, so far as working-class readers are concerned, seem to correspond with the findings of another recent research project: 'In relating culture to their job, workers alienate themselves – reading then loses what freedom, mentally liberating power, expansiveness, it possesses. The illusion that "reality" and "literature" are at opposite ends of the spectrum plays into the hands of the technocrats who encourage it. It seems as if the intelligentsia (a kind of "élite") want to keep culture as a social class preserve.' [6]

We encountered the same illusion about reality in examining the list of works read by our sample. Of course, Stendhal, Flaubert, Pavese and Marguerite Duras appeared exclusively in category *A*, while Malraux was not read 'above' category *B*. But it is difficult to establish clear-cut qualitative differences between the four reading groups – or at least the first three – for in each one a certain type of novel occupies a central place: the novel of manners, in which the story is recorded as actual experience and is combined with analysis of characters; a young man with a strong personality frees himself from a possessive mother; a doctor devoted to his patients has to overcome deep emotional conflicts; a Russian family sent into exile lives through the drama of the pre-revolutionary period. In this kind of escapist realism, which is invariably played out in a bourgeois setting, there are easily discovered digests of social and historical facts often sublimated and made rather abstract. This kind of novel occupies a fairly large place in working-class reading. It is, therefore, not enough to underline the fact that 'literature' is composed of works which structure the imaginary world in ways which parallel the social

structure of the particular historical situation,[7] still less that 'the
success of a novel indicates the existence of characteristics that a
writer has in common with his public'.[8]

One must also take into consideration the fact that fiction dedicated
to this kind of success is couched in a middling language which takes
its bearings from the ruling class and from 'official' culture while
spreading out into every social milieu. One must again emphasize that
if it is true that the structure of the novel corresponds to real social
structures, this correspondence has two aspects – one critical, the
other conformist. Some novels cut through the manifestations of
social order. Others pay due repect to them.

Our study also showed us how far the idea of the novel is mixed
up with the idea of literature. More than a fifth of the people
questioned referred to the following books as novels – *The Longest
Day*, *L'Aiglon*, a play by Courteline, *Mandingo*, an essay by Camus,
and an historical work. The existence of this confusion serves to
justify Claude Lévi-Strauss when he writes 'the fictional character
is the novel itself', in support of his contention that character has
been effaced from the contemporary novel.[9] Again, there is
MacLuhan's observation that in mass society the content of the
message is less important than the message itself, which is the
medium.[10] Reading has, in fact, become less a selective process
than a process of consumption. Reading is for reading's sake, no
more, and the word 'novel' serves to describe anything that appeals
to the imagination.

Consumption is, however, polarized on a cultural and sociological
principle of reality, accordng to which 'truth is stranger than
fiction'. Yet it is really the opposite that is true. When Truman
Capote wrote *In Cold Blood* after a patient investigation of a crime
that had fascinated the whole of America, he was making a real event
correspond to that fascination. The same applies to reports, often
noteworthy, of sociological or anthropological investigations. The
reader is made to perceive reality through the statements of the
respondents and thus he is able to discover the way in which they
represent reality to themselves. Life is made up of novelists, or of
unrecognized novels – this is the real significance of the relatively
new genre of the documentary novel, a genre which is the exact

opposite of all that Balzac stands for, since the document is made to speak for itself, instead of being shaped to form a plot.

This idea of reality is suited to a mass society whose eyes and ears are daily assailed with innumerable aspects of the world so that the imagination is clogged, instead of being inspired. The idea of society and social structures is beginning to disappear under an increasing flood of social facts, always being revised, which are represented as instances. Reading novels has become largely the reading of a fiction which is properly speaking introverted reality. It has reached a point at which it is becoming possible to write a computer programme to decide which story, based on case histories, would be most suitable for the majority of the public.

Thus it is hardly surprising that none of those we questioned regarded the novelist as an artist. He was seen as an observer, a man of experience, a moralist, an analyst of mental processes, a witness of social injustice, or merely as the man who collects the royalties. Will the sociology of the novel be content to take the place of the public, and thus occupy the place of the forces which condition sociology itself in order to produce consumer reports? Our study has been concerned with questions of meaning and form. Sociology, in our view, must also examine the relationship between artistic consciousness and social consciousness, which exists at the level of works of art themselves as well as at the level of the way in which they are received.

References

CHAPTER I

The Novel as both Literary Form and Social Institution

1. Girard, R., *Mensonge romantique et vérité romanesque*, Paris, Grasset, 1961.
2. Raimond, M., *La Crise du roman des lendemains du naturalisme aux années vingt*, José Corfi, 1965.
3. Borgès, J. L., *Discussion*, Paris, Gallimard, 1966 (French translation).
4. Barthes, R., *Writing Degree Zero*, Cape, 1967 (translation).
5. Caillois, R., *Puissances du roman*, Marseilles, 1942.
6. cf. Ford, F. M., *The Old Man: The Question of Henry James*, London, 1900; Bodley Head, 1964.
7. Brownell, W. C., *American Prose Masters*, Harvard University Press, 1923.
8. Forster, E. M., *Aspects of the Novel*, Arnold, 1927; Penguin, 1962.
9. cf. Mauriac, F., Article in *L'Express*, March 1959, and Goldmann, L., *Pour une sociologie du roman*, Paris, Gallimard, 1964.

CHAPTER 2

Sociologies of the Novel

1. Balibar, E., 'The fundamental concepts of materialism', in Althusser, L., and Balibar, E., *Reading 'Capital'*, New Left Books, 1970 (translation).
2. Proust, M., 'A propos du style de Flaubert', *Nouvelle Revue Française*, January 1920.
3. Green, Henry, *Loving*, Hogarth Press, 1945.
4. Mortimer, C., *Stranger on the Stair*, R. Hart-Davis, 1950.
5. Bowles, P., *Let It Come Down*, N.Y., Random House, 1952.
6. Macherey, P., 'L'analyse littéraire, tombeau des structures', in *Pour une théorie de la production littéraire*, Paris, Maspero, 1967.
7. Dubois, J., 'Pour une critique littéraire sociologique', in R. Escarpit *et al.*, *Le Littéraire et le social*, Paris, Flammarion, 1970.
8. Zalamansky, H., 'L'étude des contenus, étape fondamentale d'une sociologie de la littéraire contemporaine', in R. Escarpit, *Le Littéraire et le social*, op. cit.
9. James, Henry, Letter to Hugh Walpole, 19 May 1912, in *Selected Letters*, R. Hart-Davis, 1956.
10. Goldmann, L., *The Hidden God*, Routledge, 1964 (translation).
11. Goldmann, L., ibid., and *Pour une sociologie du roman*, op. cit.
12. Auerbach, E., *Mimesis*, Princeton University Press, 1953 (translation).
13. In addition to the work of Lukács, Goldmann and Macherey, there are studies by Köhler and Kardiner. Interesting critical commentaries on Goldmann's work are made by Dubois, Bonazis, Zalamansky, R. Estivals and G. Mury in *Le Littéraire et al social*, op. cit.
14. Todorov, T. and Jakobson, K., *Théorie de la littérature: textes des formalistes russes*, Paris, Editions du Seuil, 1966; Foucault, M., Barthes, R., Derrida, J., *et al.*, *Théorie d'ensemble* (Coll. Tel Quel), Paris, Editions du Seuil, 1968; Todorov, T., *Introduction à la littérature fantastique*, Paris, Editions du Seuil, 1970; Todorov, T., Preface to translation of Henry James, *Ghost Stories*, Paris, Aubier–Flammarion, 1970; Genette, G., *Figures I* and *Figures II*, Paris, Editions du Seuil 1966 and 1969; Barthes, R.,

Sur Racine, Paris, Editions du Seuil, 1963; Barthes, R., *S/Z*, Paris, Editions du Seuil; *Poétique* (literary review), 1969–70.

15. Chevalier, L., *Labouring Classes and Dangerous Classes in Paris during the First Half of the Nineteenth Century*, Routledge, 1973 (translation).

16. Foucault, M., *The Archaeology of Knowledge*, Tavistock Publications, 1972 (translation).

17. Goldmann, L., 'Introduction à une étude structurale des romans de Malraux' in Goldmann, *Pour une sociologie du roman*, op. cit.

18. Heidegger, M., *Holzwege*, Frankfurt, Klostermann, 1950.

19. Todorov, T., 'Poétique', in O. Ducrot *et al.*, *Qu'est-ce que le structuralisme ?* Paris, Editions du Seuil, 1968.

20. Genette, G., 'Métonymie chez Proust, ou la naissance du Récit', *Poétique*, 1970; Zéraffa, M., 'Thèmes psychologiques et structures romanesques dans l'œuvre de Proust', *Journal de Psychologie*, 1962.

21. Humphrey, R., *Stream of Consciousness in the Modern Novel*, Cambridge University Press, 1955.

22. Arvon, H., *Lukács*, Paris, Seghers, 1968.

23. Robbe-Grillet, A., 'Nature, humanism, tragedy', in *Snapshots*, and *Towards a New Novel*, Calder, 1965 (translation).

24. Boas, F., *Anthropology and Modern Life*, Allen and Unwin, 1929.

25. Blanchot, M., Preface to M. de Sade *Justine* and *Juliette*, Paris, Editions Tchou, 1966.

26. cf. 'Writers at Work', in *Paris Review*, New York, 1958.

27. See J. Dubois on P. Macherey's 'Pour une théorie de la production littéraire', in *La Littéraire et le social*, op. cit.

28. Meyerson, I., 'Quelques aspects de la personne dans le roman', *Journal de Psychologie*, 1951; and Zéraffa, M., *Personne et personnage: le romanesque des années 1920 aux années 1950*, Paris, Klincksieck, 1969.

CHAPTER 3

Myth and Fiction

1. Meyerson, I., 'Le temps, la mémoire, l'histoire', in special number of the *Journal de Psychologie*, 1956.
2. Vernant, J. P., *Mythe et pensée chex les Grecs*, Paris, Maspero, 1965.
3. Lévi-Strauss, C., *Mythologiques*, I, II, III, Paris, Plon, 1964, 1967, 1968. (First two volumes translated as *The Raw and the Cooked*, Cape, 1970, and *From Honey to Ashes*, N.Y., Harper Row, 1973.)
4. Vernant, J. P., op. cit.; Lévi-Strauss, C., 'The Myth of Asdiwal' (1958). English translation in E. Leach, ed., *The Structural Study of Myth and Totemism*, Tavistock Publications, ASA Monographs, 1968.
5. Frye, N., *The Anatomy of Criticism*, Princeton University Press, 1957; Weinrich, H., 'Structures narratives du mythe', in *Poétique*, 1, 1969.
6. Marichal, R., 'Naissance du roman', in *Entretiens sur la renaissance du XIIe siècle*, The Hague, Mouton, 1968.
7. Marichal, R., op. cit.
8. Marichal, R., op. cit.; Kohler, E., 'Les romans de Chrétien de Troyes', in *Revue de l'Institut de Sociologie*, Brussels, 1963; Daix, P., *Sept siècles de roman*, Editions Français Réunis, 1955.
9. Freud, S., *Wit and its Relation to the Unconscious*, Kegan Paul, 1922.
10. Robert, M., *L'Ancien et le nouveau: de Don Quichotte à Franz Kafka*, Paris, Grasset, 1963.
11. Duvignaud, J., *Sociologie du théâtre*, Paris, Presses Universitaires de France, 1965.
12. Lukács, G., *Theory of the Novel*, Cambridge, Mass., MIT Press, 1973 (translation); Lévi-Strauss, C., *Mythologiques*, III, Paris, Plon, 1968.
13. Lukács, G., *History and Class Consciousness*, Merlin Press, 1971 (translation).

14. Avron, H., op. cit.
15. Lukács, G., *Studies in European Realism* (selections in English translations). *A sociological survey of the writings of Balzac, Stendhal, Zola, Tolstoy, Gorki etc.*, Hillway Publishing Company, 1950.
16. Lukács, G., *The Meaning of Contemporary Realism*, London, Merlin Press, 1963.
17. Robbe-Grillet, A., 'The Realist Illusion', in *Towards a New Novel*, op. cit.
18. Hédelin, F. (Abbé d'Aubignac), *Macarise*, Paris, 1664.
19. Moinet, D., Introduction to J.-J. Rousseau, *La Nouvelle Héloïse*, Paris, Hachette, 1925.
20. Woolf, Virginia, *The Common Reader*, Hogarth Press, 1925; Penguin, 1938.
21. Butor, M., 'Balzac et la réalité', in *Répertoire I*, Paris, Editions de Minuit, 1960.
22. Broch, H., 'Essay on Hofmannsthal and his times', in *Dichten und Erkennen* (introduction by Hannah Arendt), Zurich, Rhein-Verlag, 1955.
23. Banuls, A., *Heinrich Mann, le poète et la politique*, Paris, Klincksieck, 1967.
24. Crémieux, B., *Inventaires: Inquiétude et reconstruction*, Paris, R. A. Correa, 1933.
25. Zéraffa, M., *Personne et personnage*, op. cit.
26. Broch, H., Essay on the *Weltanschauung* of the novel in *Dichten und Erkennen*, op. cit.
27. Astre, G.-A., *Thèmes et structures dans l'œuvre de Dos Passos*, Paris, Lettres Modernes, 1956.
28. cf. especially, G. Wasserman's preface to Hofmannsthal's unfinished *Andreas*, H. Broch, op. cit., and C. David 'Le roman de Musil', in *Preuves*, August 1958. On the Freudian view of the world, see C. Ramnoux, 'Mythe, conte et tragédie' in *Revue d'esthétique*, I, 1968, and E. Romm, 'Le modèle de l'homme chez Freud', in *L'homme et la société*, XIII, 1969.
29. cf. Eco, U., *Opera aperta: Forma e indeterminazione nelle poetiche contemporaine*, Milan, Bompiani, 1962.
30. Vernant, J.-P., op. cit.; Butor, M., 'Les Relations de parenté dans *L'ours*', in *Répertoire*, op. cit.

31. Bertaux, F., Preface to A. Döblin, *Wang-Lun* (French translation), Paris, F. Rieder, 1932.

32. Musil, R., *The Man Without Qualities*, 3 vols., Secker and Warburg, 1953–60 (translation).

33. Kettle, A., *An Introduction to the English Novel*, 2 vols., Hutchinson, 1951, 1953.

34. Kafka, F., *Wedding Preparations in the Country*, Secker and Warburg, 1954 (translation).

35. Goodman, T., *The Techniques of Fiction*, N.Y., Liveright, 1955.

36. Bellow, S., *Recent American Fiction*, Washington, U.S. Govt, Printing Office, 1963.

37. McLuhan, M., *Understanding Media*, Routledge, 1964.

38. cf. the interesting statement by M. H. Petit, 'Le renouveau picaresque dans le roman contemporain', in Colloque de Strasbourg, *Les Techniques du roman depuis* 1945, April 1970.

CHAPTER 4

The Reading of Fiction

1. 'La lecture en France', *Jeunesses littéraires de France*, Paris, 1970, no. 24.

2. ibid.

3. Orecchioni, P., 'Pour une histoire sociologique de la littérature' in R. Escarpit, *Le littéraire et le social*, op. cit.

4. Escarpit, R., ed., *Le phénomène San Antonio*, Bordeaux, Institut de Littérature et de Techniques Artistiques de Masses, 1965.

5. Robine, N., 'La lecture', in R. Escarpit *Le littéraire et le social*, op. cit.

6. Gibert, M., 'Les ouvriers et la lecture', in *Jeunesses littéraires de France*, op. cit.

7. Escarpit, R., *Le littéraire et le social*, op. cit.

8. Mury, G., 'Sociologie du public littéraire', in R. Escarpit, *Le littéraire et le social*, op. cit.

9. Lévi-Strauss, C., 'L'Origine des manières de table', in *Mythologiques* III, Paris, Plon, 1968.

10. McLuhan, M., *Understanding Media*, op. cit.

MORE ABOUT PENGUINS
AND PELICANS

Penguinews, which appears every month, contains details of all the new books issued by Penguins as they are published. From time to time it is supplemented by *Penguins in Print*, which is our complete list of almost 5,000 titles.

A specimen copy of *Penguinews* will be sent to you free on request. Please write to Dept EP, Penguin Books Ltd, Harmondsworth, Middlesex, for your copy.

In the U.S.A.: For a complete list of books available from Penguins in the United States write to Dept CS, Penguin Books, 625 Madison Avenue, New York, New York 10022.

In Canada: For a complete list of books available from Penguins in Canada write to Penguin Books Canada Ltd, 41 Steelcase Road West, Markham, Ontario.

THEORY OF LITERATURE

René Wellek and Austin Warren

This book attempts to unite poetics (or theory of literature) with criticism (evaluation), literary scholarship and history. It undertakes to arrange the main problems of literary study from the standpoint of what the authors call the 'intrinsic' concern for literature. Chapters on the nature of literature, on metre, style, metaphor, symbol, fictional technique, and genres form the core of the book, but the 'extrinsic' approaches are not slighted: literature in relation to psychology, society, ideas and the other arts is discussed at length, as are all the problems of editing and of literary history. The authors supplement each other: Mr Warren provides the sensitivity of an American New Critic, Mr Wellek the erudition and theoretical discipline of European scholarship. The peculiar success of the book lies in harmony of powers often mutually restrictive: clear theoretical vision and divers learning. The perspective is rangingly and consistently international: a panorama of modern literary scholars from America to the Slavic world is unfolded. It is an indispensable manual for every student of literature.

'It is to Richards' *Principles of Literary Criticism* that we must go for a comparable effort of clarification' – *The Times Literary Supplement*

'Should prove of the greatest value to all teachers, students, and other serious readers of imaginative literature' – *Guardian*

A PEREGRINE BOOK

LITERARY CRITICISM PUBLISHED
BY PENGUINS

Grandeur and Illusion: French Literature and Society 1600–1715
Antoine Adam

The English Novel   *Walter Allen*

The Situation of the Novel   *Bernard Bergonzi*

The Literature of the United States   *Marcus Cunliffe*

A Short History of English Literature   *Ifor Evans*

The Complection of Russian Literature   *Andrew Field*

The Rise and Fall of the Man of Letters   *John Gross*

The Truth of Poetry   *Michael Hamburger*

Tolstoy or Dostoyevsky   *George Steiner*

The Penguin Companion to Literature:

1 – British and Commonwealth Literature
2 – European Literature
3 – United States and Latin American Literature
4 – Classical and Byzantine, Oriental and African Literature